About this Learning Guide

Shmoop Will Make You a Better Lover*
*of Literature, History, Poetry, Life...

Our lively learning guides are written by experts and educators who want to show your brain a good time. Shmoop writers come primarily from Ph.D. programs at top universities, including Stanford, Harvard, and UC Berkeley.

Want more Shmoop? We cover literature, poetry, bestsellers, music, US history, civics, biographies (and the list keeps growing). Drop by our website to see the latest.

www.shmoop.com

©2010 Shmoop University, Inc. All Rights Reserved.
Talk to the Labradoodle... She's in Charge.

The Love Song of J. Alfred Prufrock
Shmoop Poetry Guide

Table of Contents

Introduction 3
   In a Nutshell 3
   Why Should I Care? 4

The Poem 4

Overview and Line-by-Line Summary 4
   Brief Summary 4
   Epigraph 6
   Stanza I 7
   Stanza II 9
   Stanza III 9
   Stanza IV 10
   Stanza V 11
   Stanza VI 12
   Stanza VII 13
   Stanza VIII 14
   Stanza IX 15
   Stanza X 16
   Stanza XI 16
   Stanza XII 17
   Stanza XIII 18
   Stanza XIV 20
   Stanza XV 21
   Stanza XVI 22
   Stanza XVII 22
   Stanza XVIII 23
   Stanza XIX 23
   Stanza XX 23

Technique 24
   Symbols, Imagery, & Wordplay 24
   Form and Meter 27
   Speaker 28
   Sound Check 28
   What's Up With the Title? 29
   Calling Card 29
   Tough-O-Meter 30
   Setting 30

Themes 31
   Theme of Love 31
   Questions About Love 31
   Chew on this: Love 31
   Theme of Manipulation 31
   Questions About Manipulation 31
   Chew on this: Manipulation 32

- Theme of Passivity 32
- Questions About Passivity 32
- Chew on this: Passivity 32
- Theme of Time 32
- Questions About Time 32
- Chew on this: Time 33
- Theme of Appearances 33
- Questions About Appearances 33
- Chew on this: Appearances 33

Quotes 33
- Love Quotes 33
- Manipulation Quotes 35
- Passivity Quotes 36
- Time Quotes 38
- Appearances Quotes 39

Study Questions 41
Did You Know? 41
- Trivia 41
- Steaminess Rating 41
- Allusions and Cultural References 42

Best of the Web 42
- Videos 42
- Audio 42
- Images 42
- Historical Documents 43
- Websites 43

Shmoop's Poetry Primer 43
- How to Read Poem 43
- What is Poetry? 45
- Poetry Glossary 47

The Love Song of J. Alfred Prufrock
Shmoop Poetry Guide

Introduction

In a Nutshell

"The Love Song of J. Alfred Prufrock" is totally a modernist poem.

Whoa, whoa, hold on there a sec – what's this all about?

OK, so you might have heard of a little movement called "modernism." Nobody out there has a great definition of modernism, but here's ours. For most of history, most people lived really far away from one another in small villages. They didn't travel much or interact with one another. This is the pre-modern world. Then, along come all these new technologies – everything from sewer systems to railroads – and suddenly lots of people are living close together in cities, and even those who aren't living close together are able to find out what's going on with the help of (from oldest to most recent) telegrams, newspapers, telephones, cell phones, and the internet. Welcome to the modern world – but, of course, you were here already, Mr. or Mrs. Internet User.

Nowadays, we're all used to living in the modern world, but it wasn't always that way. The "modernists" basically include all the artists and writers who were living smack in the middle of the huge, massive transformation from olden days to modern times, which was roughly the end of the 19th century to the middle of the 20th century. In their work, they try to make sense of all these changes, which no one quite understands. Got it?

So "The Love Song of J. Alfred Prufrock" is totally a modernist poem. Its author, T.S. Eliot, was an American who moved to Britain in 1914. Eliot wrote most of "Prufrock" when he was 22 years old (!), in the years before the start of World War I. At that time, Britain was considered the most modern country in the world. The poem is set in a big, dirty city, and its speaker is a very unhappy man who is afraid of living and therefore bored all the time. War, cities, boredom, and fear: these are all classic modernist themes.

Eliot got "Prufrock" published in *Poetry* magazine in 1915 with the help of his buddy Ezra Pound, who was like a friendly uncle-figure to a lot of the European modernists. In 1917 it was published as part of a small book called *Prufrock and Other Observations*.

It was considered pretty experimental at the time, and a lot of people hated it. The "Literary Supplement" of *The London Times* had this to say: "The fact that these things occurred to the mind of Mr Eliot is surely of the very smallest importance to anyone, even to himself. They certainly have no relation to poetry…" *Times Literary Supplement* 21 June 1917, no. 805, 299). A lot of people still hate the poem, mostly because they had it pounded into them by overly strict teachers in school, which is the quickest way to suck the fun out of anything. Fortunately, Eliot has fallen a bit out of style lately, so now's the perfect time to pick up the poem and decide for yourself how you feel about it.

After the publication of "Prufrock," Eliot went on to publish some of the most important poems of the 20th century, including "The Wasteland," his best known. He was awarded the Nobel Prize for Literaturein 1948.

Why Should I Care?

First off, we've got to address the haters.

Garrison Keillor, a humorous newspaper columnist and radio host, has called "Prufrock" "a small, dark mope-fest of a poem." He writes: "This poem pretty much killed off the pleasure of poetry for millions of people who got dragged through it in high school" (source).

This is a standard reaction to many of T.S. Eliot's poems. You, too, may be in the process of being dragged through the poem in one of your classes. It would definitely be a chore to have to find all of Eliot's smarty-pants references to classic works of literature, and, read from a certain angle, the poem is pretty dark. BUT…we also think this is one of the funniest works of the century. Come on, it's about a skinny, bald guy who talks in nursery rhymes and wishes he were a crab. Forget Eliot the bookworm; this is Eliot the wicked satirist, poking fun at "the man."

If he had wanted to, Eliot could have written a *really* mopey poem. Considering the time he was writing, it would have made perfect sense. "Prufrock" was published during World War I, one of the most violent conflicts in human history. It was not a time to write about birds and flowers. But instead of crying into his British ale, he wrote a hilariously pointed attack on all the well-dressed, upstanding citizens who loved their material pleasures – their tea and marmalade – more than they loved other people.

Most of all, reading "Prufrock" should make you want to drop everything and go tell your secret crush about your feelings for him or her. It's a warning to all procrastinators: if you put something off once, you'll likely put it off forever. Don't be like Prufrock and focus on the worst-case scenario. And, if you do score a date with your secret crush, whatever you do, don't take him or her to a "sawdust restaurant with oyster shells." We hear the atmosphere leaves something to be desired.

The Poem

You can find "The Lovesong of J. Alfred Prufrock" on Poets.org.
(http://poets.org/viewmedia.php/prmMID/20220)

Overview and Line-by-Line Summary

Brief Summary

Meet Prufrock. (Hi, Prufrock!). He wants you to come take a walk with him through the winding,

The Love Song of J. Alfred Prufrock
Shmoop Poetry Guide

dirty streets of a big, foggy city that looks a lot like London. He's going to show you all the best sights, including the "one-night cheap hotels" and "sawdust restaurants." What a gentleman, he is! Also, he has a huge, life-altering question to ask you. He'll get to that later, though.

Cut to a bunch of women entering and leaving a room. The women are talking about the famous Renaissance painter Michelangelo. We don't know why they're talking about Michelangelo, and we never learn. Welcome to Prufrock's world, where no one does anything interesting.

Did we mention that it's foggy. Like really, really foggy. The fog has a delightful yellow color, and it acts a lot like a cat.

Yawn. What a day. We've accomplished so much already with Prufrock. There's still a lot of stuff he still wants to get done before "toast and tea." People to see, decisions to make, life-altering questions to ask. But not yet…There's still plenty of time for all that later.

Where did the women go? Oh, yes, they're still talking about Michelangelo.

Yup. Pleeeen-ty of time for Prufrock to do all that really important stuff. Except that he doesn't know if he should. He's kind of nervous. You see, he was about to tell someone something really important, but then he didn't. Too nervous. Oops! At least he's a sharp-looking guy. Well, his clothes are sharp-looking. The rest of him is kind of not-so-sharp-looking. People say he's bald and has thin arms.

But he still has pleeen-ty of time. And he's accomplished so much already! For example, he has drank a lot of coffee, and he's lived through a lot of mornings and afternoons. Those are pretty big accomplishments, right? Plus, he's known a lot of women. Or at least he's looked at their hairy arms, and that's almost as good.

Prufrock says something about how he wishes he were a crab. Oh, Prufrock! Always the joker. Wait, you were serious? That's kind of sad, my friend. Don't you have important things to do?

Oops! It looks like he didn't do that really important thing he meant to do. He was going to tell someone something life-altering, but he was afraid of being rejected. So he didn't. Oh well.

Meanwhile, Prufrock keeps getting older. He doesn't worry about that really important thing anymore. Instead, he worries about other important things, such as whether to roll his pant-legs or eat a peach.

It turns out that Prufrock really likes the ocean. He says he has heard mermaids singing – but they won't sing to him. Boy, you sure do talk a lot about yourself, Prufrock. Finally, he brings us back into the conversation. He talks about how we lived at the bottom of the sea with him (geez, we don't remember that one!). It turns out we were asleep in the ocean, but all of a sudden, we get woken up by "human voices." Unfortunately, as soon as we wake up, we drown in the salty ocean. Boy, what a day. We thought we were talking a walk, and now we're dead.

The Love Song of J. Alfred Prufrock
Shmoop Poetry Guide

Epigraph

S'io credesse che mia risposta fosse
A persona che mai tornasse al mondo,
Questa fiamma staria senza piu scosse.
Ma perciocche giammai di questo fondo
Non torno vivo alcun, s'i'odo il vero,
Senza tema d'infamia ti rispondo.

- The epigraph of this poem is a six-line quotation from Canto 27 of the *Inferno* by the Renaissance Italian poet Dante Alighieri.
- And no, Eliot doesn't translate it out of the Italian, which is the kind of stunt that makes people think Eliot is a snob. We really can't defend him on this charge, except to say that he was absolutely and totally obsessed with Dante and maybe he thought other people loved Dante as much as he did – enough to translate the quote for themselves.
- Sneaky little references to Dante pop up *everywhere* in Eliot's poems, but this one is more obvious – it's a direct quotation.
- The *Inferno* tells the story of how a guy (Dante) who has messed up his life badly enough to require some help from the nice folks in heaven. In order to scare him away from sin and other bad things, heaven sends another poet named Virgil to give Dante a guided tour through the horrors of Hell (known as "Inferno" in Italian). Along the way he meets a lot of evil and misguided people.
- The quote from this epigraph is said by one of the characters in the eighth circle of Hell (which has nine circles), where some of the worst of the worst are stuck for eternity. This particular guy's name is Guido da Montefeltro, and when Dante asks to hear his story, here's what he says:
- "If I thought that my reply would be to someone who would ever return to earth, this flame would remain without further movement; but as no one has ever returned alive from this gulf, if what I hear is true, I can answer you with no fear of infamy."
- What does this quote mean? Well, Dante is really curious to know why Guido ended up so far down in Hell. But Guido is selfish. He's afraid that people back on earth will find out about the horrible stuff he did – he's concerned about his reputation.
- On the other hand, Guido knows that no one has ever entered Hell and made it out again, so he figures that it's safe to tell his story because Dante is stuck here.
- Unfortunately for Guido, Dante is the first human ever to be allowed to pass through Hell and "return to earth," so people do eventually find out about Guido's sins…from reading the *Inferno*.
- One other thing we should mention: Guido doesn't even have a body in Hell – he's not worthy of that – so his entire spirit is just a "flame" that "moves" when he talks. When he says, "this flame would remain without further movement," he means, "I would shut up and not talk to you anymore."
- Last thing: What did Guido do? Essentially, Guido committed terrible atrocities in war.
- But that's not the worst part. The worst part is that he tried to have himself forgiven *before* he committed these atrocities. He basically thought he could out-smart God and get into heaven despite doing things that he knew were really bad. It's like if before you broke your mother's favorite lamp you asked her, "Mom, if I broke this lamp right now, would you forgive me? . . . Yes? OK." CRASH!

The Love Song of J. Alfred Prufrock
Shmoop Poetry Guide

- (Note to Guido: You can't outsmart the creator of the universe.)
- Why does Eliot choose this epigraph for his poem? Well, it suggests a couple of things. First, that "Prufrock" might not be a poem about good people, but about bad ones pretending to be good. The setting of the poem is a kind of hell.
- Second, it tells us that this fellow Prufrock, who is singing his "love song," might be concerned about his reputation like Guido. In other words, Prufrock is going to tell us things because he thinks we won't have a chance to repeat them to other people.

Stanza I

Lines 1-3
LET us go then, you and I,
When the evening is spread out against the sky
Like a patient etherised upon a table;

- "We" are being invited on a trip somewhere. Oh, fun!
- But who am "I"? Am I the reader of "J. Alfred Prufrock," or am I someone else? For the purposes of the poem, you are someone else.
- Right from the very start, by addressing itself to a fictional person, the poem is announcing that it's a "dramatic monologue." We know that a "dialogue" is two people talking, so a "monologue" must be one person talking, because "mono" means "one." The poem is "dramatic" because it is written in the voice of a speaker other than the poet.
- We know this from the title, which tells us that the speaker is a guy named J. Alfred Prufrock – this is his song. (In olden times, poems were called "songs").
- It's not clear who Prufrock is singing to, but the title gives us a hint. Love songs are usually sung to people you're in love with, so it's a safe bet that Prufrock is addressing someone he loves.
- Because these were more traditional times, we'll assume this "someone" is a woman. Also, just to liven things up a bit, let's pretend that we, the readers of the poem, are the woman he loves. Feel free to giggle now if you want.
- Prufrock tells us the time of day that we're taking this trip: evening. But, this is not your ordinary evening: this "evening" is "spread out against the sky like a patient etherised upon the table."
- Holy cow! What does that mean?
- Really, it's hard to overstate how shocking this opening was to readers of Eliot's time. We're still a bit shocked ourselves. It's one of the most famous opening images – ever.
- The image compares the evening sky to a patient strapped to an operating table and given ether, a kind of anesthetic, to numb the pain of the surgery that is about to happen. (In case you were wondering, the word is pronounced: *ee*-thur-ized). It's an amazing, jarring, outrageous image.
- *This* is how you start a love song? You suckered us into taking an evening stroll, Prufrock, and now it's like we're about to watch a gory surgery happen. Give us a moment to calm down.

Lines 4-7

Let us go, through certain half-deserted streets,
The muttering retreats
Of restless nights in one-night cheap hotels
And sawdust restaurants with oyster-shells:

- Prufrock repeats his invitation for us to come along with him. One of things you'll notice about this poem is that it repeats itself a lot.
- Now, usually when you go on a walk with someone, especially someone you love, you try to pick someplace romantic – a moonlit beach, a tree-lined avenue, that sort of thing. Not Prufrock. He's going to take us through "half-deserted streets," where people walk around "muttering" to themselves.
- Hm. These are the kind of streets that are filled with "cheap hotels" where you might stay for one night only as a last resort, if you had no other options.
- Well, at least the street has "restaurants."
- Actually, these are the kind of restaurants that have "sawdust" on the floor to clear up all the liquor that people are spilling as they start to get drunk. It's also littered with oyster-shells that no one bothers to clean up.
- Eliot is sending us a lot of small signals in this section. "Half-deserted" makes the streets sound pretty sketchy, and "one-night cheap hotels" only adds to this impression. "Oysters" are an aphrodisiac, which means, to put it bluntly, that they make people want to have sex…
- Oh dear. It looks like Prufrock has taken us on a stroll through the seedy red-light district, where prostitutes and vagrants hang out.
- Remember the epigraph, which comes from Dante's *Inferno*? Well, we're in a different kind of hell – the underbelly of a modern city.

Lines 8-12

Streets that follow like a tedious argument
Of insidious intent
To lead you to an overwhelming question …
Oh, do not ask, "What is it?"
Let us go and make our visit.

- The streets twist and turn like a "tedious argument." It's an argument with "insidious intent" – the streets are so confusing it's as if they were trying to trick us into getting lost.
- But, by this point, we might feel that Prufrock is also being "insidious" by trying to trick us into taking a walk through the seedy part of town.
- We could even go a step further and say that both the streets and Prufrock resemble Guido da Montefeltro, who tried to fool God (see "Epigraph").
- The streets are leading somewhere, however. They lead "to an overwhelming question," a question of huge and possibly life-altering significance.
- Oh, tell us, tell us!
- Nope, Prufrock isn't going to tell us, and he doesn't even want us to ask what it is. If we

The Love Song of J. Alfred Prufrock
Shmoop Poetry Guide

want to find out, we're going to have to take a walk with him. Sounds pretty tricky, if you ask us.
- For good measure, he repeats his favorite phrase, "let us go," for a third time. Seriously, folks, when people warn you about bad peer-pressure situations, this is what they mean.

Stanza II

Lines 13-14
In the room the women come and go
Talking of Michelangelo.

- There's not much to explain about what's going on in these lines. Women are entering and leaving a room talking about the Italian Renaissance painter Michelangelo.
- Eliot loves those Italians. The quote is adopted from a poem the 19th century French writer Jules Laforgue, but that doesn't really help us figure out what it means here.
- And, no, you're not missing anything – these lines really do come out of nowhere and seem to have nothing to do with Prufrock's question.
- They do, however, add to the general atmosphere. For one thing, the women must be pretty high-class to be talking about Renaissance art, but their repeated action of "coming and going" seems surprisingly pointless.
- Remember how we said that Eliot includes sneaky references to Dante *everywhere*? Well, Dante's Hell features a lot of really smart people who repeat utterly pointless physical gestures over and over again in small, cramped spaces. Just something to think about.
- Finally, these lines have an incredibly simple, singsong rhyme that could get really annoying if you had to listen to it for a long time. It sounds like a nursery rhyme, which totally doesn't fit with the intellectual subject of famous painters.

Stanza III

Lines 15-22
The yellow fog that rubs its back upon the window-panes,
The yellow smoke that rubs its muzzle on the window-panes
Licked its tongue into the corners of the evening,
Lingered upon the pools that stand in drains,
Let fall upon its back the soot that falls from chimneys,
Slipped by the terrace, made a sudden leap,
And seeing that it was a soft October night,
Curled once about the house, and fell asleep.

- It appears that the poem is back to talking about the "half-deserted streets" from stanza I.

The Love Song of J. Alfred Prufrock
Shmoop Poetry Guide

- The streets are filled with a "yellow fog," which sounds really nasty, actually. This detail might allow us to take a stab at the location of the poem.
- Eliot was really interested in England, and he moved there before this poem was published. The capitol of England is London, which gets really foggy. You've probably heard the phrase, "London fog."
- So maybe we're in London. Around the beginning of the 20th century, London was a really modern city that also had some of the roughest, seediest neighborhoods anywhere.
- This fog seems pretty acrobatic. It has a "back" and a "muzzle," which sounds like either a dog or a cat. Also, it "licks" things and makes "sudden leaps." OK, definitely sounds like a cat.
- The poem is comparing the quiet, sneaky, and athletic movement of the fog to a common housecat. It's a pretty sweet image. If you've ever been around a cat, you know how they can sneak up on you. One moment you're sitting on the couch, reading a book, and the next moment, something soft and furry is rubbing against your leg.
- The fog is wandering around the streets like a cat wanders around a house.
- Finally, the fog gets tired and "curls" around the city houses to "fall asleep" like a cat would curl around something smaller, maybe the leg of a table or chair.
- One interesting detail: it's a "soft October night," which means the poem is set in autumn.

Stanza IV

Lines 23-25
And indeed there will be time
For the yellow smoke that slides along the street,
Rubbing its back upon the window-panes;

- Eliot knew a *lot* about literature. He read more books than almost any other writer in the 20th century – maybe more than any other writer, period. He could make subtle references to all kinds of literary figures without even trying. His brain worked like that. Good for him.
- But you don't have to "get" these references to understand his poems. Sometimes, though, they are fun to point out.
- Here, the phrase "there will be time" refers to a poem called "To His Coy Mistress" by the 17th century English poet Andrew Marvell.
- "To His Coy Mistress," like many poems, is about a man trying to get a woman to sleep with him, and it begins: "Had we but world enough, and time, / This coyness, lady, were no crime." The woman is being "coy" by pretending that she won't sleep with the poet. The poet is saying, "Look, we both know you want to sleep with me, and if we had until Eternity to be together, it would be fine for you to waste time playing games. But we don't, so let's hop to it."
- Prufrock, however, uses the reference to "time" in exactly the opposite way. He thinks there's plenty of time for delays and dawdling.
- Just like in Marvell's poem, Prufrock addresses himself to a "mistress," someone he "loves," but here it's Prufrock, and not the mistress, who is being "coy."

- By talking about the smoke, he's trying to justify the fact that he wasted our time with an entire stanza of description of the fog instead of asking that "overwhelming question" he told us about.

Lines 26-34

There will be time, there will be time
To prepare a face to meet the faces that you meet;
There will be time to murder and create,
And time for all the works and days of hands
That lift and drop a question on your plate;
Time for you and time for me,
And time yet for a hundred indecisions,
And for a hundred visions and revisions,
Before the taking of a toast and tea.

- He keeps repeating that "There will be time," as if he hasn't quite convinced himself, or his lover.
- Plenty of time to get your "face" ready to meet other people. Also, plenty of time to "murder and create," which sounds pretty sinister. Is this supposed to be a good thing or a bad thing? We're not sure.
- In the next line, he says there's "time for all the works and days of hands." Allusion alert: *Works and Days* was the name of the name of a work written by the Greek poet Hesiod. It's poem about the importance of working for a living and not living a lazy a pointless existence.
- Hmm…pointless existence…sounds like someone we know, eh, Prufrock?
- Also, have you noticed how Prufrock seems to refer to individual body parts instead of people? So far we have "faces" and "hands." The hands are dropping a "question" onto a "plate," as if it were something we could dig into like a fancy steak dinner. Bring it on!
- But no, we still don't learn what the question is.
- Plenty of time for that later. There's also time for "indecisions," for not deciding things. We have all this time "before the taking of a toast and tea."
- Now this *really* seems like England, doesn't it?

Stanza V

Lines 35-36

In the room the women come and go
Talking of Michelangelo.

- This lines seem to "come and go" from the poem just like the women they describe. Hello, women! Goodbye, women!

The Love Song of J. Alfred Prufrock
Shmoop Poetry Guide

Stanza VI

Lines 37-39
And indeed there will be time
To wonder, "Do I dare?" and, "Do I dare?"
Time to turn back and descend the stair,

- There's still plenty of time to do all the important things Prufrock wants to do, except now he's second-guessing himself.
- The setting gets more specific, too. We might imagine him standing outside the upstairs room his "love" is in. He paces back and forth and tries to decide whether to ask his big question. "Do I dare?" he wonders. But no, he doesn't dare. He turns around and heads back downstairs.
- Of course, Prufrock doesn't exactly describe this scene to us: he's much too tricky for that. Instead, he poses it as a hypothetical situation – "Well, if I wanted to chicken out and not ask my question, there's plenty of time for that, so what's the big deal?"
- Sure there's time, Prufrock, sure there is.

Lines 40-44
With a bald spot in the middle of my hair—
[They will say: "How his hair is growing thin!"]
My morning coat, my collar mounting firmly to the chin,
My necktie rich and modest, but asserted by a simple pin—
[They will say: "But how his arms and legs are thin!"]

- Now he's going to describe his appearance, and the first thing we learn is he has a big bald spot. He's probably a middle-aged man, or at least close to it.
- Also, he seems worried about what people will say about him and his bald spot and his thin arms and legs.
- His only attractive features, funny enough, are his clothes. He has a nice coat and necktie, which he wears according to the fashion of the time. He's not a trend-setter, though, he's a trend-follower.
- As for "they," we don't know who "they" are, but according to Prufrock, they're a gossipy bunch – and not so nice.
- Prufrock's concern about what other people think might make us suspicious. Back to the Epigraph we go!
- Recall that Guido da Montefeltro was also worried about his reputation, even though it didn't matter because he was already in hell.
- Prufrock, too, seems to have nothing to lose by asking his question – it's not like we were in love with the guy already. To the contrary, he seems like kind of a coward. But now, on top of cowardice, he also seems superficial.

The Love Song of J. Alfred Prufrock
Shmoop Poetry Guide

Lines 45-48
Do I dare
Disturb the universe?
In a minute there is time
For decisions and revisions which a minute will reverse.

- Prufrock doesn't want to rock the boat or "disturb the universe." That would involve taking a risk, and risks aren't Prufrock's thing.
- But he still insists (again) that he has plenty of time. Truth be told, he's starting to sound pretty kooky, like a broken record.
- Even though he hasn't done anything in the poem yet, he insists that everything could change "in a minute" – if only he could make a decision.
- But things can also change back again in another "minute," once he "revises" the decision he made. Kind of like when he was about to enter the room to tell his love something, and then went back down the stairs.
- But, Prufrock, doesn't that just leave you where you started?

Stanza VII

Lines 49-54
For I have known them all already, known them all:—
Have known the evenings, mornings, afternoons,
I have measured out my life with coffee spoons;
I know the voices dying with a dying fall
Beneath the music from a farther room.
So how should I presume?

- Now he's trying to convince us that he's a wise man with lots of experience. He doesn't need to do anything, because he's done everything already!
- And by "done everything," we mean he has survived "evenings, mornings, afternoons." Impressive.
- What else have you done, Prufrock? Well, he has drank a lot of coffee – in fact, his whole existence can be "measured" by how much coffee he has drank.
- This is a wicked image. Prufrock thinks he is impressing us, but he's really damning himself before our eyes. He basically lives from one cup of coffee to the next, with nothing interesting in between.
- Prufrock says he has heard voices "dying" or fading away when music starts to play in a "farther room." We already know that he has a hard time entering rooms that contain people he wants to talk to (see lines 37-39), so he has to settle on overhearing other people's voices through the walls. He lives through other people.
- The phrase "dying fall" is, you guessed it, another literary reference, this time to

The Love Song of J. Alfred Prufrock
Shmoop Poetry Guide

Shakespeare's famous play, *Twelfth Night*. In the first scene of the play, a lovesick count named Orsino is listening to music that has a "dying fall." The music reminds him of his love for one of the other characters.

- In this poem, however, it's as if Prufrock were overhearing the "voices" of another couple – maybe Orsino and his love? – in another room, which get covered up by yet another room even "farther" away.
- It's a tricky image, we know, but the point is that Prufrock can only experience love at second- and third-hand. If Orsino's love is the real thing, then Prufrock's is just a copy of a copy of a copy.
- Finally, he asks, "So how should I presume?" To "presume" is to take for granted that something is the case. The speaker of Andrew Marvell's " To His Coy Mistress" presumes that his mistress wants to sleep with him.
- This can be a bad thing, if you presume *too much*, but Prufrock is just looking for any reason not to ask his important question. He doesn't want to "presume" that he'll get a favorable response. This is pretty cowardly of him.

Stanza VIII

Lines 55-56

And I have known the eyes already, known them all—
The eyes that fix you in a formulated phrase,

- Here he goes with the body parts again – this time it's "the eyes." The guy has seen a lot of eyes in his time. (Are we supposed to be impressed?)
- He's trying to cover up his fear but not doing a very good job.
- He doesn't like how eyes seem to "fix" or freeze him, and a "formulated phrase" means a phrase that judges, summarizes, and reduces something complicated to something simple. We don't know what phrase he has in mind, but it shouldn't be surprising by now that he's afraid of judgments of any kind by other people.

Lines 57-61

And when I am formulated, sprawling on a pin,
When I am pinned and wriggling on the wall,
Then how should I begin
To spit out all the butt-ends of my days and ways?
And how should I presume?

- Oh my. Now he's really starting to lose it. He's starting to confuse his verb tenses. He just told us that he has "already" known the eyes that would formulate him, but now he talks as if this event hasn't happened yet. Which is it, Prufrock?
- We're starting to think he hasn't really "known" anything at all.

The Love Song of J. Alfred Prufrock
Shmoop Poetry Guide

- He imagines himself "sprawling on a pin" and put, "wriggling," on a wall.
- He's referring to the practice, in his time, where insects that were collected by scientists were "pinned" inside a glass frame and hung on a wall so they could be preserved and inspected. If you go to a really old science museum, you can sometimes see examples of these insect specimens.
- So Prufrock is imagining that the eyes are treating him like a scientist treats an object of study. He doesn't like that so much.
- The image of a guy tied down and "wriggling" might also remind you of the very first lines of the poem, when the evening was "spread out" like a patient on the operating table.
- Prufrock seems pretty spooked by doctors and scientists – maybe because these people can see things for what they really are.
- He thinks that once these scientific eyes have got a hold on him, he'll have to talk about or rather "spit out" the story of his life ("days and ways").
- The "butt-ends" could refer to any kind of end – the little odds and ends of his daily life, the evenings he spent, etc. But it's also the word people use for the end of a cigarette, the part that doesn't get smoked. Prufrock is comparing his life to a used-up cigarette.
- Oh, and, by the way, he's still worried about "presuming" too much about the situation. Thanks for the reminder, Mr. P.

Stanza IX

Lines 62-64
And I have known the arms already, known them all—
Arms that are braceleted and white and bare
[But in the lamplight, downed with light brown hair!]

- Considering how much he dislikes scientific observation of himself, he sure does it a lot to other people. Here he sees women merely as "arms," and he uses the same repetitive phrase about how he has "known them all."
- He sounds tired and bored, as if he were saying, "If I have to see *one more* white arm with a bracelet on it . . .!"
- But he seems pretty excited about the arm in line 64. This is probably the arm of the woman he invited on a walk (the "you" of the poem).
- If they did go for a walk through half-deserted streets, it would make sense to see her arm under the "lamplight." The soft, "light brown hair" makes this arm different from all the other ones and would seem to contradict his claim to have seen *all* the arms.

Lines 65-66
It is perfume from a dress
That makes me so digress?

The Love Song of J. Alfred Prufrock
Shmoop Poetry Guide

- Finally! Just when we were wondering where the heck this poem was going, Prufrock admits that he has been "digressing," or wandering away from the main point.
- And what is that main point? We're not sure anymore: that's how far he has digressed.
- He blames his digression on the scent of a woman's perfume. For a guy that claims to have known all the women, he's still fairly preoccupied with all things feminine.

Lines 67-69
Arms that lie along a table, or wrap about a shawl.
And should I then presume?
And how should I begin?

- Lots of arms. Loooots of arms. It reminds us of Dr. Seuss's "Green Eggs and Ham." "Did you see them in a shawl? Did you see them down the hall?"
- Oh, and in the off chance that you forgot, he still doesn't know whether he should "presume" to do something.
- He still hasn't told us what that something is. He doesn't even know where to "begin" talking about it.

Stanza X

Lines 70-72
Shall I say, I have gone at dusk through narrow streets
And watched the smoke that rises from the pipes
Of lonely men in shirt-sleeves, leaning out of windows?...

- Here he wonders how to "begin" to talk about that difficult subject. And the difficult subject is...himself! Oh, brother.
- This is the story of his "days and ways" from line 60, and it begins "I have gone at dusk through narrow streets."
- But, of course, we know that already. He's basically taking us back to the beginning of the poem. The most interesting new detail he has to offer us is that he saw "lonely men" smoking pipes out of their windows.
- Some people bring the party with them wherever they go; Prufrock brings the loneliness with him.

Stanza XI

Lines 73-74

The Love Song of J. Alfred Prufrock
Shmoop Poetry Guide

I should have been a pair of ragged claws
Scuttling across the floors of silent seas.

- Here's another image from way out of left field. It might also be the most accurate self-evaluation that Prufrock offers in the entire poem.
- It would have been more fitting, he says, to have been born as a pair of crab claws that "scuttle" across the floor of the ocean.
- The crab is the perfect image of Prufrock, because it seems suited to a single over-riding goal: self-protection.

Stanza XII

Lines 75-78
And the afternoon, the evening, sleeps so peacefully!
Smoothed by long fingers,
Asleep ... tired ... or it malingers,
Stretched on the floor, here beside you and me.

- Prufrock continues to confuse the past, present, and future. He winds the clock back to the afternoon and then plays it forward to the evening, which is when we started the poem.
- The afternoon and evening are "sleeping," much as the cat-like fog was asleep outside the house in line 22. He's wondering if he should "wake" the day up somehow, say, by asking (cough, cough) a certain question? But he's hesitant because the day seems so peacefully asleep, as if it were being "smoothed by long fingers."
- This image of the fingers makes us think of petting a cat, but it may remind you of something different. The evening is "asleep" and "tired" – nothing is happening. But it might also be "malingering," or pretending to be tired.
- At any rate, it looks pretty comfortable stretched out there on the floor – and, hey, there's "you" again! We haven't seen the second person for quite some time. Nice of you to mention us, Prufrock.

Lines 79-80
Should I, after tea and cakes and ices,
Have the strength to force the moment to its crisis?

- Well, some time must have passed in the poem, because "tea" is over. In line 34, he hadn't had tea yet, but now he's digesting all the sweet and tasty things he consumed.
- It must be a pretty easy life for Prufrock, what will all the eating and doing nothing.
- He's feeling so lazy, in fact, that's he's not sure he has the "strength" to ask the "overwhelming question," which would produce a big decision or a "crisis."

The Love Song of J. Alfred Prufrock
Shmoop Poetry Guide

Lines 81-83
But though I have wept and fasted, wept and prayed,
Though I have seen my head [grown slightly bald] brought in upon a platter,
I am no prophet—and here's no great matter;

- Prufrock doesn't want to be confused with a prophet. (We want to tell him: "Don't worry, no danger of that!") Even though he weeps, fasts, and prays like a prophet, he isn't one. Even though, um, he has seen his head on a platter – what's that about?
- In the Bible, the prophet John the Baptist, who baptized Jesus, dies after the stepdaughter of a powerful king asks for his head on a platter.
- We're not sure what Prufrock is trying to say – he may just be feeling sorry for himself.
- He doesn't want us to think he feels sorry for himself, though – he says it's "no great matter." But if we lost our head, we would probably beg to differ.

Lines 84-86
I have seen the moment of my greatness flicker,
And I have seen the eternal Footman hold my coat, and snicker,
And in short, I was afraid.

- He continues to mope around and feel sorry for himself. He already feels as if his best days are behind him, like a candle that flickers and goes out.
- In the old days (even older than Eliot's poem), a "footman" was like a butler who would help rich people do things. One of the things a footman would do is to hold your coat as you got in a carriage or entered a house.
- But this footman isn't so friendly. He's the eternal Footman – "death" – and if he's holding your coat, it means you are probably about to enter some place that you won't come out of again.
- Prufrock has another rare moment of honesty when he admits to being afraid. It's pretty uncommon for him to say anything "in short" like that.

Stanza XIII

Lines 87-93
And would it have been worth it, after all,
After the cups, the marmalade, the tea,
Among the porcelain, among some talk of you and me,
Would it have been worth while,
To have bitten off the matter with a smile,
To have squeezed the universe into a ball

The Love Song of J. Alfred Prufrock
Shmoop Poetry Guide

To roll it toward some overwhelming question,

- Time in the poem continues to play tricks on us. Now Prufrock talks as if he has already passed up on his opportunity to do that important thing.
- He starts this big long thought about whether "it would have been worth it," which he won't finish until the end of the stanza, so just keep this thought in mind.
- It seems that even more eating and drinking have been going on, as well as "some talk of you and me," which suggests that "we" have been having tea with our dear Prufrock.
- He talks about "biting off the matter," as if it were something he could eat, like his precious marmalade (a kind of jam). "The matter," we assume, is the important thing that he meant to discuss so many lines ago.
- He compares the effort it would required to take on "some overwhelming question" to squeezing the entire universe into a ball. Sounds pretty hard, but do we believe him?

Lines 94-95
To say: "I am Lazarus, come from the dead,
Come back to tell you all, I shall tell you all"–

- Prufrock compares his task of asking the question to Lazarus coming back from the dead. Really, now, this is a bit much. It shouldn't take a resurrection to tell someone how you feel.
- But there's more to the story. In the Bible, a rich man named Dives dies and gets sent to Hell. Around the same time, a poor man named Lazarus dies and gets sent to Heaven. Dives asks the prophet Abraham to please send Lazarus back to earth to warn his brothers to mend their ways or they'll end up in Hell. Abraham is like, "No way, man. If your brothers didn't get the message already, what with all the prophets and such who have been running around, one dead guy coming back to life isn't going to save them."
- Now, ahem: (Pointing our finger, Batman-style) to the Epigraph! The epigraph comes from a poem about another guy who, unlike Dives, *did* make it back from Hell to tell warn people about sin. His name was Dante Alighieri, the poet.
- But Prufrock is no Lazarus, nor is he a Dante. He's more like Dives, the guy who never escapes from his terrible situation.

Lines 96-98
If one, settling a pillow by her head,
Should say: "That is not what I meant at all.
That is not it, at all."

- Now he finally completes the sentence, "Would it have been worth it, after all," from the beginning of the stanza. The sentence goes, "Would it have been worth it, after all, if one, settling a pillow by her head, should say: 'That is not what I meant at all. That is not it, at all.'"
- Clearly Prufrock thinks that, no, it would not have been worth it. So, he thinks, it's a good

The Love Song of J. Alfred Prufrock
Shmoop Poetry Guide

- thing he never tried or risked anything.
- Prufrock is imagining his worst-case scenario: he has asked her his big question – though we still don't know what it is – and she replies that she has been misunderstood.
- But why would the woman with the pillow think she has been misunderstood?
- Maybe his question is something like, "I'm really into you, and when you did such-and-such thing, it made me think you were into me, too. Do you want to kick it with me?" But that's just a wild guess.
- At any rate, he never asked the question, because he was too afraid of getting rejected. So he'll never know if that's what she "meant."

Stanza XIV

Lines 99-104
And would it have been worth it, after all,
Would it have been worth while,
After the sunsets and the dooryards and the sprinkled streets,
After the novels, after the teacups, after the skirts that trail along the floor –
And this, and so much more? –
It is impossible to say just what I mean!

- He's still thinking in worst-case-scenario mode. He wonders if it would have been worth it if after him and his love have experienced all of these nice but trivial pleasures of everyday, middle-class life, including "sunsets," "novels," and "teacups" – but he can't finish his thought.
- If we had to guess, we might say that he's afraid that if his big question didn't go over well, it would throw a wrench in his tidy, polite, inoffensive life. It's the most bogus excuse in the book, like when you ask someone on a date and they say, "No, I don't want to ruin our friendship."
- But Prufrock is right about one thing: he's totally incapable of saying what he means.

Lines 105-110
But as if a magic lantern threw the nerves in patterns on a screen:
Would it have been worth while
If one, settling a pillow or throwing off a shawl,
And turning toward the window, should say:
"That is not it at all,
That is not what I meant, at all."

- Ah, now he comes up with the right words to say what he means. It's as if the words locked in his "nerves" were being projected by a "magic lantern" onto a screen for him to read.

- But, in typical Prufrock-fashion, even the right words are disappointing. It's just another image of a woman sitting on a couch or a bed and saying she has been misunderstood.
- Once again, it is implied that he doesn't think asking her would have been worth the risk of rejection.
- But, once again, he'll never know, will he.

Stanza XV

Lines 111-119

No! I am not Prince Hamlet, nor was meant to be;
Am an attendant lord, one that will do
To swell a progress, start a scene or two,
Advise the prince; no doubt, an easy tool,
Deferential, glad to be of use,
Politic, cautious, and meticulous;
Full of high sentence, but a bit obtuse;
At times, indeed, almost ridiculous –
Almost, at times, the Fool.

- Aside from Dante, the poet whom Eliot loved most was Shakespeare. So here's a Shakespeare reference.
- In *Hamlet*, the title character is an indecisive chap, much like Prufrock has been for most of the poem. Hamlet can't decide whether or not to kill his uncle, even though his uncle has committed some really awful crimes. Like Prufrock, Hamlet can seem like a coward who talks too much. But now Prufrock says he's not like Hamlet, after all.
- And if you like puns, the end of line 111 has a good one. In the play, Hamlet begins his most famous speech: "To be or not to be, that is the question." You might even say it's an "overwhelming question." But Prufrock has already made a decision on that question: he was not "meant to be."
- Prufrock compares himself to a minor character in the play, one of the "attendants" who serve the king. We think he's talking about Polonius.
- In *Hamlet*, Polonius is the father of Ophelia, the heroine, and everyone respects him because he always takes the cautious route and acts like "an easy tool." Even Shakespeare uses him to "start a scene or two" in the play, then kills him off around the midway point.
- Polonius talks a good game – he uses fancy words ("high sentence") and proverbs – but in the end, he's kind of a dunce. As Prufrock so cautiously puts it, he's "almost ridiculous" and almost like "the Fool."
- With this recognition, Prufrock has finally arrived at a pretty honest assessment of himself. It's a bit late, however, to do anything about it. It's never good to just say, "Yeah I'm a tool, but, oh, well."

The Love Song of J. Alfred Prufrock
Shmoop Poetry Guide

Stanza XVI

Lines 120-121
I grow old ... I grow old ...
I shall wear the bottoms of my trousers rolled.

- Ah, yes. We love these lines because they bring some silliness back into the poem. Trousers. Ha!
- Though Prufrock has done a pretty good job so far at disguising the passage of time, he can no longer hide the fact that he's getting older and older. He blew his chance to ask the question, and now he's like the guy who stays at a party too long, except that the party is his own poem.
- Because he already failed to make one big decision, he's going to pretend he's an assertive, confident guy by making a bunch of comically minor decisions. Thus, the infamous rolled trousers bit. A true classic.
- Hey, at least his pant-legs won't get wet if he steps in a puddle. Always thinking ahead, that Prufrock.

Stanza XVII

Lines 122-123
Shall I part my hair behind? Do I dare to eat a peach?
I shall wear white flannel trousers, and walk upon the beach.

- As one of the annotated guides to Eliot's poems put it, parting your hair behind was considered "daringly bohemian" at the time.
- Prufrock is still trying to make all kinds of tiny decisions, now that he has missed his big chance. As always, he's interested in the small pleasures of food and fashion, like the peach and the white flannel trousers.
- He's also going to check out the ocean – maybe he'll talk about how he wants to be a crab again.

Line 124
I have heard the mermaids singing, each to each.

- OK, so no crabs. Instead, he sees some mermaids.
- Wait, that's actually pretty exciting. But this is Prufrock, who can't keep track of what time it is, so he says he has "heard" the mermaids singing to each other, as if this event were already in the past.

The Love Song of J. Alfred Prufrock
Shmoop Poetry Guide

Stanza XVIII

Line 125
I do not think that they will sing to me.

- Even the mermaids won't sing to him. Where's your self-confidence, man!

Stanza XIX

Lines 126-128
I have seen them riding seaward on the waves
Combing the white hair of the waves blown back
When the wind blows the water white and black.

- Of all the things Prufrock claims to have seen, the mermaids are definitely the coolest.
- But do we believe him? He has tricked us before.
- These mermaids look like they're surfing on the waves with their tails. The only troubling sign is that the waves have "white hair," which makes us think of old people.

Stanza XX

Lines 129-131
We have lingered in the chambers of the sea
By sea-girls wreathed with seaweed red and brown
Till human voices wake us, and we drown.

- This is kind of an "it was all a dream" ending, but even weirder.
- Prufrock brings "us" back into the picture, saying that we have been hanging out in the ocean with him.
- The word "chambers" has two meaning here: it can refer to small cramped spaces, or it can refer to rooms, especially bedrooms.
- Remember that Prufrock has spent significant amounts of time lurking outside of rooms and imagining women who are wrapped in shawls and laying on pillows. We don't know who the "sea-girls" are, but they don't seem quite as majestic as the mermaids.
- The "human voices" may remind us of the "voices with a dying fall" from line 52.
- Oh, and by the way, we're dead. We drowned with Prufrock. No!
- Seriously, though, we can't help you much with this ending. It could signal that Prufrock

The Love Song of J. Alfred Prufrock
Shmoop Poetry Guide

has truly grown insane, or that his "true self" is really more crab-like that human, or that, yes, he has been dreaming the whole time. (We don't really buy the dream story, but if that's your thing, go for it.)
- One thing is clear: Prufrock's story does not turn out well. It does not turn out well, at all.

Technique

Symbols, Imagery, & Wordplay

Welcome to the land of symbols, imagery, and wordplay. Before you travel any further, please know that there may be some thorny academic terminology ahead. Never fear, Shmoop is here. Check out our "How to Read a Poem" section for a glossary of terms.

Sinister Streets

The poem begins with Prufrock inviting us to take a walk with him, but we soon learn that this isn't some romantic tree-line avenue by the river. Quite the opposite, it seems to be the seediest part of town. True to Prufrock's circular and evasive style, the poem returns several times to the imagery of these gritty streets, with contrast with the prim and proper middle-class life he seems to lead. Just like our narrator, the streets are misleading and go nowhere.
- Lines 4-7: Parts of the scene are depicted using personification. It's not the "retreats" that are "muttering," but it seems that way because they are the kinds of places where you would run into muttering people. Also, the nights aren't actually "restless"; they make people restless.
- Lines 8-10: In this simile, the winding, twisting streets are compared to a "tedious argument" that makes people lost with confusion. An "argument" is a line of reasoning – lawyers make arguments, for example. Usually arguments are supposed to answer questions, but this one only leads to "an overwhelming question."
- Lines 13-22: An extended metaphor comparing the streets to a cat runs through this entire stanza. Prufrock never actually uses the word "cat," but it's clear from words like "muzzled," "back," "tongue," "leap," and "curled" that he is talking about a sly little kitty.
- Line 64: The lamplight from the same streets reveals the hair on the woman's arm.
- Lines 70-72: Prufrock returns to the setting of the beginning of the poem to give the imagery of a man leaning out of a window and smoking a pipe.

Eating and Drinking

Have you ever seen one of those PBS shows or period films where British people sit around and sip tea and eat finger foods? "Prufrock" offers a parody of this easy-going tradition, as Prufrock thinks constantly about what he has just eaten, what's he's about to eat, or what he may or may not eat in the future. Especially tea. He's a total caffeine junky, which may explain why he seems to talk so much. It's one of those small daily pleasures he just can't live without.
- Line 7: Most of the food and drinks in this poem sound nice, but not the oysters at this low-class restaurant. There's even sawdust on the floor to soak up all the spilled drinks.

The Love Song of J. Alfred Prufrock
Shmoop Poetry Guide

- Line 34: Prufrock has big plans to accomplish before "toast and tea" in the afternoon.
- Line 51: In this famous metaphor, Prufrock says that the spoons he uses to measure his coffee are like a "measure" of his life, as well. Here the spoon is a synecdoche that actually refers to the whole process of sitting around in the afternoon and sipping on a nice, hot, caffeinated drink. Essentially, he lives from one cup of coffee or tea to the next.
- Line 81: It's very ironic for Prufrock to claim he has fasted, considering that we know how much toast and marmalade he likes to eat. What nerve!
- Lines 89-90: The cups, marmalade, tea, and porcelain all refer, once again, to Prufrock's favorite pastime. Did somebody say "tea time!"
- Line 91: It seems that Prufrock has trouble thinking of anything except eating. Here he discusses "the matter" of his big question using the metaphor of taking a bite.
- Line 122: Before Prufrock was wondering whether he "dared" to ask his question. Now that the opportunity has slipped by him, he has other important things to worry about: such as whether to eat a peach. (Just eat the darned thing, man).

Body Parts

Prufrock is very concerned about his reputation, and he doesn't want to stick out in a crowd. He'd rather people not notice him at all, which is why he seems uncomfortable with doctors and scientists, whose jobs involve examining and taking things about. But he's also like a scientist himself in the way that he "cuts people up" (yikes) in his mind, reducing people, and especially women, to a collection of body parts. He loves to use the "synecdoche," which takes one part of an object and uses it to represent the whole. He talks about "faces," "eyes," and "arms," but never full human beings.

- Lines 2-3: Although it doesn't directly deal with body parts, the simile comparing the evening to a patient who has been put under anesthesia ("etherised") on a surgery table prepares us for all the metaphorical "surgery" and "dissecting" that Prufrock does when he sees people only as body parts.
- Lines 27-29: The "faces" are a synecdoche; you don't go out just to meet a face, you go out to meet the entire person.
- Lines 40-44: Prufrock's "bald spot" is a repeated symbol of his middle age, just as his nice clothes are a symbol of his relatively high social class. Unfortunately, the clothes are only good feature (that we know of). Indeed, he also has thin arms and legs. Which is surprising, because the guy eats all the time.
- Lines 55-58: Again, the eyes are a synecdoche – they are a part of a person used to stand for the whole person. After all, eyes can't "formulate," only a thinking person can do that. He uses the metaphor of a scientist examining an insect specimen to describe the way he feels under the gaze of those critical "eyes."
- Lines 62-67: Sigh, here we go again. The arms are a part that stands for a whole – in this case, a whole woman. Synecdoche!
- Line 82: Prufrock gets decapitated! The poem just turned into a Quentin Tarantino movie. Actually, we're not sure what he means here, except that he is making a metaphorical allusion to John the Baptist from the Bible, whose decapitation is regarded as an example of Christian sacrifice. Prufrock is comparing his own sacrifice to John's.

The Love Song of J. Alfred Prufrock
Shmoop Poetry Guide

The Ocean
Prufrock suggests that he might be better suited to living in the deep, cold, lonely ocean than in the society of other people. We think he's on to something. But when he ends up in the ocean through some crazy, dream-like turn events at the end of the poem, he doesn't do very well. In fact, he drowns.
- Lines 73-74: The "claws" are synecdoche. They stand for a crab, which is the animal you'd most likely think of as "scuttling" on the ocean floor. Prufrock is calling himself crab-like.
- Line 123-131: The poems ends with some amazing ocean imagery, including the singing mermaids and the sea-girls wearing seaweed. In one of the poem's most creative metaphors, the white-capped waves are compared to "white hair."

Rooms
Prufrock spends most of the poem cooped up in rooms, eating, drinking, and overhearing other people's conversations. He also fantasizes a lot about entering rooms – perhaps bedrooms – where the woman he loves can be found. Always the pessimist, he images a woman leaning on a pillow who rejects him. At the end of the poem, he just might have found the perfect room for him: at the bottom of the ocean.
- Lines 13-14, 35-36: These lines are one of the most famous refrains in a poem with many of 'em. These verses are repeated in exactly the same form twice in the poem.
- Lines 38-39: We know that Prufrock is inside of a house – and probably standing outside a room – when he tries to decide whether to go in. He chickens out, though, and he's back downstairs.
- Lines 52-54: The "dying fall" of voices from another room is an allusion to Shakespeare's *Twelfth Night*. Count Orsino, one of the lovers in that play, refers to the "dying fall" of music that reminds him of his love. Therefore, it is ironic, when the voices Prufrock hears are covered up by "music from a farther room."
- Lines 75-79: The afternoon/evening is personified as a person who is sleeping alongside Prufrock and his fictional listener in a room after "tea and cakes and ices."
- Lines 107-110: The woman in Prufrock's imagined worst-case scenario must be in a room of some kind, probably a bedroom or some other comfortable place. She lays on a pillow and turns to the window.
- Line 129: "Chambers" is a word that can refer to any small space – like the "chambers" of the heart muscle – or it can refer specifically to a bedroom.

Hamlet
Prufrock spends much of the poem acting like the notoriously indecisive Hamlet. But, in the end, he decides that even indecision is too decisive for him. No, he's more like an assistant to a lord – a guy who does nothing but follow orders and generally acts like a tool.
- Lines 111-119: In this important metaphor, Prufrock likens himself to Prince Hamlet, the title character from Shakespeare's most famous play. But then he decides he's actually more of an "attendant lord" who could be confused for a fool, which we think is an allusion

to Polonius, the father of the character Ophelia in the same play.

Form and Meter

Dramatic Monologue
A dialogue is a conversation between two people, but a monologue is just one person talking. ("Mono" means "one). But "Prufrock" is a "dramatic" monologue because the person talking is a fictional creation, and his intended audience is fictional as well. He is talking to the woman he loves, about whom we know very little except for the stray detail about shawls and hairy arms.

A good dramatic monologue gradually reveals more and more about the person speaking, without them intending to reveal so much. At the beginning Prufrock is just a slightly creepy guy who wants to take a walk. As the poem goes on, we learn about his personal appearance, his love of food and fashion, and his desire to be a pair of crab claws. The impression we get about him is exactly the opposite of the one he wants to give. He wants us to think that he's a decision-maker, a "decider," if you will, who dresses well and seizes opportunities when they come. But he's just a big fraud. He never decides anything, and when he misses his big opportunity, he tries to pretend it's no biggie.

So, the overarching form is the dramatic monologue, but if you look closer at the poem, you'll find that Eliot is experimenting with all kinds of forms and meters. For example, there are a lot of rhyming couplets, like the first two lines, and the famous verse about the women and Michelangelo.

We think that Eliot is making fun of Prufrock by using this old-fashioned form. The rhyming couplets are sometimes called "heroic" couplets, but our title character is anything but heroic. The rhymes also have a singsong quality that makes them seem childish. He rhymes "is it" with "visit"? Come on. But this is Prufrock's song, and Eliot is just pulling the strings to make him look bad – quite masterfully, we might add.

Other lines don't rhyme and sound more like free verse, which has no regular meter. Occasionally we'll get a couple of lines of blank verse, which have no rhyme but a regular meter, usually iambic pentameter, where an unstressed syllable is followed by an accent. This is the meter that Shakespeare used most often, and Eliot was a huge fan of Shakespeare. Thus, "I SHOULD have BEEN a PAIR of RAG-ged CLAWS."

Shakespeare also used rhyming couplets in iambic pentameter, and, lo and behold, this it the form we get in lines 111-119, which discuss Shakespeare's *Hamlet*. Using Shakespeare's verse to talk about Shakespeare? T.S., you clever man.

Speaker

Prufrock
There are at least three sides to our speaker, Prufrock. On one side we have the sneaky trickster, who invites us on a romantic walk only to lead us down windy roads and point out that the evening looks like a patient about to undergo surgery. He keeps stalling and leading us away from the main subject (his "overwhelming question"), as if he had something to hide. And he constantly confuses the time of day and even the past versus the future, like a casino manager who removes all the clocks from the building so customers won't realize they have someplace else to be.

On the other side we have Prufrock the Fool, whose desperate attempts to make us think he's a cool, confident ladies' man is comically transparent. Really, who is this guy think he's kidding?

Finally, we have the sad, honest man who realizes the jig is up and can't even convince himself of his own stories. This Prufrock, who only lets his mask drop for a few lines at a time, is the one who admits that he should have been "a pair of ragged claws" and that he has seen "the moment of [his] greatness flicker" (lines 72, 84). Like a juggler, the poem keeps a delicate balance between these three personalities, so that one never gets an upper hand other the others.

Our speaker is an average middle-class man. In fact, we think that if you put a bunch of Prufrocks together in a room, you would have "The Man," that mysterious killjoy who secretly controls the world. He doesn't want to rock the boat, and he is most concerned with keeping the status quo, which means nice clothes, fine tea, and utter boredom all the time. He wields power in society but has no power of his domestic life. He kind of suspects that he's a "ridiculous" and a "Fool" but could never fully admit it to himself (lines 118-119). This is a poem where we get to put "The Man" under the microscope and watch him squirm.

There's one part of the poem, however, that isn't in the voice of Prufrock. This is the Epigraph. We think the Epigraph is Eliot's little joke on Prufrock, and a warning to those who have read Dante (or who care to look up the reference) that we shouldn't trust everything we hear.

Sound Check

Eliot was kind enough to provide us with the perfect metaphor for the sound of this poem. It's the cat-like fog that pads around the city in endless circles (lines 13-22). Eliot's verses are very cat-like, and they keep circling around Prufrock without ever letting us see him head-on. Sometimes the verses rub their "muzzle" or "back" against the real Prufrock, but we only see him faintly, as through a fog.

Like a Siamese cat, Eliot is an exceptionally athletic and agile poet. He can go from rhymed to unrhymed verses without you even knowing it. With feline slyness, the poem slips in and out of blank verse, and it also makes "sudden leaps," like when it suddenly transitions from Prufrock to

The Love Song of J. Alfred Prufrock
Shmoop Poetry Guide

the women talking of Michelangelo and back again.

The circling pattern is both obvious and maddening. The poem repeats the same refrains over and over and, like "how should I presume?" and "there will be time." You could find yourself dizzy from all this circling. Sometimes we think we're getting close to the center of the circle, like when Prufrock wonders, "Do I dare?" But then the poem just leads us back out again, and the motion continues.

The poem's simple rhymes, like a nursery song, create a foggy confusion that distracts us from the sinister or "insidious" intent of the speaker (line 9). Watch how all these tricks come together in the following verses: "In a minute there is time / For decisions and revisions which a minute will reverse" (lines 47-48). The first line leads us to an expectation – time for what!? – which the second line "reverses." The ridiculously obvious internal rhyme of "decisions" and "revisions" blinds us to the fact that the poem has not told us *what* has been decided and *what* has been revised. Every time you try to get your hands on this quick little cat, it slips away from you. This is a poem where you should keep your eyes open to what's really going on – otherwise, you could get lost in the fog.

What's Up With the Title?

The original title of this poem wasn't "The Love Song of J. Alfred Prufrock." It was – ready for this? – "Prufrock Among the Women." We're glad Eliot changed his mind about this original title, which sounds like a terrible 1950's musical. But it does tell us that Eliot thinks Prufrock's relation to the fairer sex is at the center of this poem. "Love Song" makes a similar point, but not as directly.

The title is actually the only place where Prufrock's name is mentioned – in the poem he talks about himself in the first person. Eliot is clearly poking fun of himself with this title – as a young man he signed his name "T. Stearns Eliot," but that doesn't mean the poem is biographical. For one thing, we're pretty sure Eliot didn't drown in the ocean. The other thing to know about the title is that it's completely ironic in light of the poem, which is not so much a "love song" as the depressed ramblings of a lonely and cowardly man. If you have ever seen *The Daily Show* or one of the other "fake news" programs, then you know the kind of irony that's at work here. The title of the poem is only pretending to be serious, while the poem itself is more like a "fake love song."

Calling Card

Hidden Literary Allusions
In poems like "The Waste Land," Eliot takes the time-honored principle of literary name-dropping to a whole new level. The poem has footnotes, for Pete's sake! "Prufrock" gives only a sample taste of Eliot's encyclopedic knowledge of literature. The Epigraph is from Dante's *Inferno*, and references to several other works, from Shakespeare's *Twelfth Night* and *Hamlet* to Hesiod's *Works and Days*, to Andrew Marvell's "To His Coy Mistress," are inserted

so casually into the text that you could easily miss them. Which is OK. Eliot was a playful thief of the words and ideas of other poets, and he would probably be amused to know the extent to which stuffy scholars have taken these allusions as the "key" to understanding his works. As with all poetry, there is no "key."

Tough-O-Meter

(7) Snow Line
Eliot frightens people more than almost any other poet. Like other modernists, he sometimes uses foreign language in his poems, and here we get an Epigraph in Italian. He also slips in sly references to writers from Shakespeare to Hesiod. But, seeing as this poem is about deception, being confused is part of the point. If you read it slowly, Eliot gives all the clues you need to figure out Prufrock's little game.

Setting
We start this journey in a dark, smelly neighborhood of London. It's October. Steam is rising from the streets, and a sick yellow fog circulates around the crooked houses. Drunks are stumbling out of the "sawdust restaurants" and sloppy-looking couples argue outside of "cheap hotels." A woman with bright clothes and too much makeup is leering at you from her doorway. And all the while Prufrock is there besides you, gesturing for you to follow him further down this rabbit-hole of squalor and darkness . . . Pretty soon you're both lost, which was just what he intended.

Part of the poem takes place in this obviously hellish part of the big metropolis. But the poem's other setting is just as bad, though it looks nicer on the surface. This is the London of the tired and bored middle-class, sitting in their cramped rooms drinking tea and coffee all day. All anyone seems to do is lie around and grow older. In other parts of the house, people are talking and laughing and music is playing, but we're not allowed to go in there…Prufrock offers you yet another cup of coffee, and you don't even know what time of day it is. If you eat one more "cake" you think you'll explode. Prufrock is getting older before your eyes – his hair turns white and his arms get even thinner.

Out of nowhere, he takes us to the beach. (Finally! Our skin was getting pasty from all that staying indoors.) Look, mermaids! This is the nicest thing we have seen all day. But suddenly things get all disoriented and the world turns upside down. We're at the bottom of the sea, surrounded by girls wrapped in seaweed. We hear voices, wake up, and…uh-oh.

The Love Song of J. Alfred Prufrock
Shmoop Poetry Guide

Themes

Theme of Love

It's hard to tell whether Prufrock is really in love with the person he is talking to. He speaks about himself *a lot*, and he ignores her, or "us," for most of the poem. Maybe he's too shy to speak his mind, although "cowardly" seems more accurate. There are a couple of points where he almost overcomes his massive fear of rejection, especially when he is standing on top of the stairs and wondering, "Do I dare?" (line 38). But he's so vain and so taken up with trivial pleasure like coffee and peaches that it's hard to believe that the feeling he has is really "love." It might just be lust or just a strong attraction. Whatever it is, the feeling never goes anywhere, and Prufrock is left to drown with his would-be beloved in the deep, deep ocean.

Questions About Love

1. Is the title accurate in calling the poem a "love song"? Do you think Prufrock is really in love?
2. At what points in the poem does he seem more interested in love, and at what points does he not seem to care?
3. What is the real reason that Prufrock never asks his "overwhelming question"?
4. Prufrock imagines that his love would say, "That is not what I meant at all." What would she be responding to, and what did he think she "'meant."

Chew on this: Love

Prufrock is not just some stalker. He truly believes his beloved has sent him signals that she likes him, but he is worried that he might be misinterpreting her signals.

Prufrock can only experience love through other people, at second- and third-hand.

Theme of Manipulation

The poem's epigraph is a quotation of Guido da Montefeltro, a particularly manipulative chap who finds a place near the bottom of Dante's Hell in *Inferno*. Right away, this epigraph sets off alarm bells that we should be suspicious of everything that shy old Mr. Prufrock says. First he's trying to lead us down dark, winding streets, then he's trying to convince us of how decisive he is. Prufrock is one of the most deceptive narrators you'll ever encounter.

Questions About Manipulation

1. Guido da Montefeltro only told Dante the story of his life because he thought Dante would not return to earth to repeat it. Is Prufrock doing the same thing in this poem?
2. Do you think Prufrock is lying outright about some of his claims, or is he just misleading?
3. How does the structure of the poem play to Prufrock's advantage?
4. If Prufrock is so manipulative, then why is it so easy for a reader to see through his

deception?

Chew on this: Manipulation
Prufrock purposefully arranges his song to leave out all the parts that would make him look bad.

Although Prufrock says he is not prophet, he's really the prophet of the so-called "modern man."

Theme of Passivity
Oh, Prufrock, why didn't you just go into your lover's "chamber" and ask her your darned "overwhelming question" when you had the chance?! Prufrock is the dramatic equivalent of a bump on a log. He never does anything. In this poem, no one does. Actions are discussed as either future possibilities or as thing already done and past. And not for a second do we believe that Prufrock has "known" all the things he claims to have known. The only thing this guy is good at is eating and wearing nice clothes.

Questions About Passivity

1. Why does Prufrock "turn back and descend the stair" instead of entering the next room?
2. What kinds of things does Prufrock claim he has done? Are any of them impressive or noteworthy?
3. How does Prufrock pretend to be more assertive than he is?
4. Can passivity alone make someone a bad person?

Chew on this: Passivity
The entire poem is one big, long digression so that Prufrock doesn't have to tell his life story.

Prufrock's passivity is dangerous because it makes him hold tightly to the status quo. He is willing to go to great lengths to prevent things from changing.

Theme of Time
In relation to time, this poem is a total trip. It ricochets back and forth between the past and the future, almost never settling on the present. One moment Prufrock is talking about all the things he's going to do before having tea; the next moment he has had tea and still doesn't have the energy to do anything. But somehow, by the end of the poem, Prufrock's big chance has passed him by, and he becomes a sad, old man in flannel pants.

Questions About Time

1. Where does the poem begin, and where does it end? Are these points at different times?
2. How many events actually "happen" over the course of the poem?

3. At what points does the poem seem to go back in time?
4. How would you explain these lines: "In a minute there is time / For decisions and revisions which a minute will reverse"?

Chew on this: Time

No time actually passes over the course of the poem.

"Prufrock" must be set in Hell because people repeat the same thoughts and actions over and over, like someone running in place.

Theme of Appearances

There seem to be no complete human beings in this poem. There are only bits and pieces of people: an arm here, some eyes there, maybe a couple of voices in the next room. The person whose appearance we know most about is Prufrock, and we kind of wish we hadn't learned about his bald spot or his bony arms and legs. The lack of bodies is one of the signs that might make us think the poem is set in Hell.

Questions About Appearances

1. Why is so much attention paid to clothing in the poem?
2. Why does Prufrock get so excited by the arm with "light brown hair" that he sees under the lamplight?
3. What do we know about the appearance's of the woman Prufrock loves? Do you think the same woman is being described over and over?
4. Why are there descriptions of "mermaids" and "sea-girls" at the end of the poem?

Chew on this: Appearances

Although Prufrock mistrusts doctors and scientists, he acts like one when he "dissects" people in his perception.

Prufrock is more like a strange sea-creature than a man.

Quotes

Love Quotes

LET us go then, you and I,
When the evening is spread out against the sky
Like a patient etherised upon a table; (lines 1-3)

The Love Song of J. Alfred Prufrock
Shmoop Poetry Guide

Thought: The first two lines sounds line a tender invitation, perhaps to take a moonlit stroll or a walk on the beach. Then BAM! the third line totally explodes the romance, and we realize this is not an ordinary "love song." Prufrock compares the evening to a patient that is about to undergo a painful surgery. For an audience in Eliot's time, this must have been a shocking way to start a poem. The grim tone fits the times, however: "Prufrock" was published in 1915, when the bloodiest war in history up to that point, WWI, was well underway, and "ether," an anesthetic, was in high demand for use on injured soldiers.

And indeed there will be time
To wonder, "Do I dare?" and, "Do I dare?"
Time to turn back and descend the stair,
With a bald spot in the middle of my hair – (lines 37-40)

Thought: It seems like Prufrock is oh-so-close to asking his question, as he wonders "Do I dare?" We imagine he's standing by a door, on the other side of which is the woman he loves. He's pacing back and forth, deciding whether to knock and enter. In the end, though, he's too afraid, and he heads back downstairs. He tries to play it cool and claim "there will be time" for all his indecisiveness, but, in reality, this was his big chance, and he blew it.

I know the voices dying with a dying fall
Beneath the music from a farther room.
So how should I presume? (lines 52-54)

Thought: Prufrock lives through other people, so he only "knows" love by listening to the voices of people in other rooms, which get muffled by music. By using the phrase "dying fall," he echoes Count Orsino, one of the great lovers from Shakespeare's *Twelfth Night*. If Prufrock hadn't "turned back" in line 39, it could have been his voice whispering sweet nothings on the other side of the wall. But he was too worried about "presuming," or reading too much into the situation with the woman he loves.

And I have known the eyes already, known them all –
The eyes that fix you in a formulated phrase,
And when I am formulated, sprawling on a pin,
When I am pinned and wriggling on the wall,
Then how should I begin
To spit out all the butt-ends of my days and ways? (lines 55-60)

Thought: We don't know whose "eyes" he means, but it's likely they belong to one or several of the women he has loved. They intimidate him and make him feel like he is being examined like a scientist examines an insect specimen. He doesn't want to have to tell the truth about himself ("my days and ways") to anyone, even someone he thinks he loves.

The Love Song of J. Alfred Prufrock
Shmoop Poetry Guide

And I have known the arms already, known them all –
Arms that are braceleted and white and bare
[But in the lamplight, downed with light brown hair!]
It is perfume from a dress
That makes me so digress? (lines 62-66)

Thought: Prufrock sounds really jaded, like a kid who has been on an amusement ride too many times. He's seen so many arms it makes his head spin. But wait! Look at that arm over there, in the lamplight. That's a mighty nice arm, "downed with light brown hair." And the "perfume" is making him ramble on and on. Here for about two seconds, he actually sounds like a man who might be in love, or at least lust. At this point, we would take lust over nothing.

I do not think that they will sing to me. (line 125)

Thought: Prufrock has already realized that his best days over, but now he finally comes to terms with the fact that no one will love him. And it's all his own fault for not doing anything about it. He sees the beautiful mermaids singing in the water, but he has no confidence that they would even turn his way. Still, he doesn't drop his guard and sounds pretty matter-of-fact about his total undesirability.

Manipulation Quotes

S'io credesse che mia risposta fosse
A persona che mai tornasse al mondo,
Questa fiamma staria senza piu scosse.
Ma perciocche giammai di questo fondo
Non torno vivo alcun, s'i'odo il vero,
Senza tema d'infamia ti rispondo. (epigraph)

Thought: Yes, we feel bad about using a quote in Italian, but if it makes you feel better, we'll give the translation: "If I thought that my reply would be to someone who would ever return to earth, this flame would remain without further movement; but as no one has ever returned alive from this gulf, if what I hear is true, I can answer you with no fear of infamy." This is Guido da Montefeltro speaking to the poet Dante Alighieri in Hell (go back to the Detailed Summary if you need more info). The quote basically shows that Guido is only talking about himself because he thinks no one will find out. It shows us he's pretty much a manipulative toad, which should raise our suspicions about the poem that follows.

Streets that follow like a tedious argument
Of insidious intent
To lead you to an overwhelming question …
Oh, do not ask, "What is it?"
Let us go and make our visit. (lines 8-12)

The Love Song of J. Alfred Prufrock
Shmoop Poetry Guide

Thought: Even the streets are trying to mislead us. They have an "insidious intent," which means they are wind all over the place and will likely make us lost...A lot like the poem. Come to think of it, all of Prufrock's arguments are fairly "tedious," too. You could change the word "streets" to "verses" and it would perfectly fit this "love song."

And indeed there will be time
To wonder, "Do I dare?" and, "Do I dare?"
Time to turn back and descend the stair,
With a bald spot in the middle of my hair – (lines 37-40)

Thought: You'd think that Prufrock was narrating something that actually happened here, or that is actually happening: he wants to go tell someone something, but he chickens out and runs for the exit. But by putting the line, "And indeed there will be time" in front of this little story, he turns it into a hypothetical situation, one that may or may not have happened. This is one of the places we learn not to trust this guy.

For I have known them all already, known them all: –
Have known the evenings, mornings, afternoons,
I have measured out my life with coffee spoons; (lines 49-51)

Thought: When he says he has "known them all," he wants us to think that he's an old hand at life. Been there, done that. He doesn't need new or exciting experiences, because he has had them already. But what exactly is he claiming to have done? Lived through different times of day with the help of a lot of caffeine? Any exhausted student cramming for an exam can tell you what's that's like – and it's hardly the time of your life.

I grow old … I grow old …
I shall wear the bottoms of my trousers rolled. (lines 120-121)

Thought: He's starting to run out of steam at this point. He's like an actor who has to stay on stage even after the play ends. But that's not going to stop him for convincing us that he's "The Decider!" He even makes big decisions like rolling his pant-legs. Sounds like a super-hero to us.

Passivity Quotes
In the room the women come and go
Talking of Michelangelo. (13-14)

Thought: Although these lines don't add to Prufrock's story (or lack thereof), the image of these women coming and going while talking about a famous Renaissance painter totally captures the passivity of the poem. It's not like they are looking at paintings or taking a class or something. They're just talking about old stuff in a room that isn't described at all.

The Love Song of J. Alfred Prufrock
Shmoop Poetry Guide

And indeed there will be time
For the yellow smoke that slides along the street,
Rubbing its back upon the window-panes;
There will be time, there will be time
To prepare a face to meet the faces that you meet;
There will be time to murder and create,
And time for all the works and days of hands
That lift and drop a question on your plate;
Time for you and time for me,
And time yet for a hundred indecisions,
And for a hundred visions and revisions,
Before the taking of a toast and tea. (lines 23-34)

Thought: Prufrock has big plans. BIG plans. And there's plenty of time to accomplish them all before tea is served. He has time to spend an entire stanza talking about the fog. Also, he has time to get ready and "prepare a face" to meet other people. Kind of weird, but OK. We're not so sure about "to murder and create," though. That could be hard to get done before tea, unless he has a getaway car planned already. But there's definitely time for "a hundred indecisions." If anyone is capable of not making a decision, it's our man Prufrock.

So how should I presume? (line 54)

Thought: This is just one of the many stall-tactics that Prufrock uses to put of asking his question or saying anything important at all. He justifies all his delays because he doesn't want to "presume," or act like something is the case when it may not be. But what he really means is he doesn't want to take a risk by sharing his thoughts or feelings.

And the afternoon, the evening, sleeps so peacefully!
Smoothed by long fingers,
Asleep ... tired ... or it malingers,
Stretched on the floor, here beside you and me.
Should I, after tea and cakes and ices,
Have the strength to force the moment to its crisis? (lines 75-80)

Thought: Here he's just lazing around, like a kid on summer holiday, eating sweet foods and trying not to "wake up" the afternoon/evening, which is being personified as a sleeping person. It's hard to tell whether the evening is really tired, though, or if it's just "malingering," or faking it to get out of doing something important. Kind of like Mr. Lazy Bones over there with his "tea and cakes." He's like the kid who promises to do the dishes after dinner and then after dinner complains, "But I'm too tiiiired!" He doesn't have the "strength" to do anything that make cause a stir.

The Love Song of J. Alfred Prufrock
Shmoop Poetry Guide

No! I am not Prince Hamlet, nor was meant to be;
Am an attendant lord, one that will do
To swell a progress, start a scene or two,
Advise the prince; no doubt, an easy tool,
Deferential, glad to be of use,
Politic, cautious, and meticulous;
Full of high sentence, but a bit obtuse;
At times, indeed, almost ridiculous –
Almost, at times, the Fool. (lines 111-119)

Thought: In literature, Hamlet is a classic example of a passive character. He spends all his time thinking about whether to murder his uncle, and he never gets around to doing anything about it. But Prufrock is even worse than Hamlet. He's more like an "attendant lord" who serves a king. Everybody is nice to him, but nobody respects him because he doesn't want to cause trouble for anyone, including himself. In other words, Prufrock is saying that he's not even the main character in his own story.

Time Quotes

In the room the women come and go
Talking of Michelangelo. (lines 13-14)

Thought: These lines are the first clue that we might be in a timeless "Twilight Zone." The woman come and go, come and go, and they are always talking. Their repetitive motion is like listening to a broken record or watching the same scene over and over again. This is a lot like Dante's *Inferno*, where characters repeat the same pointless motions endlessly as punishment for leading small, meaningless lives.

And indeed there will be time
For the yellow smoke that slides along the street,
Rubbing its back upon the window-panes;
There will be time, there will be time
To prepare a face to meet the faces that you meet;
There will be time to murder and create,
And time for all the works and days of hands
That lift and drop a question on your plate;
Time for you and time for me,
And time yet for a hundred indecisions,
And for a hundred visions and revisions,
Before the taking of a toast and tea. (lines 23-34)

Thought: Prufrock echoes Andrew Marvell's poem " To His Coy Mistress," in which the poet tries to convince a woman to hop into bed with him because, he says, they don't have eternity to sit around and play games. But Prufrock believes the opposite: he thinks he can keep stalling and delaying forever, and that there is plenty of time for games and "indecisions." He's the

The Love Song of J. Alfred Prufrock
Shmoop Poetry Guide

ultimate procrastinator. Of course, if we imagine Prufrock as being trapped in something like Dante's Hell, then he *would* actually have eternity to sit around and hesitate – but that's not such a good thing.

In a minute there is time
For decisions and revisions which a minute will reverse. (lines 47-48)

Thought: One minute he was about to say something really important to the woman he loves, the next minute he "revised" his decision and went back downstairs. Strangely, he uses his own failure to act as a reason to *keep stalling*. There's plenty of time to not make a decision, he says, because you can always make it later on. Of course, if you keep insisting there is plenty of time forever . . . you get the point.

And the afternoon, the evening, sleeps so peacefully!
Smoothed by long fingers,
Asleep ... tired ... or it malingers,
Stretched on the floor, here beside you and me.
Should I, after tea and cakes and ices,
Have the strength to force the moment to its crisis? (lines 75-80)

Thought: Prufrock keeps confusing the past and the future throughout the poem – maybe on purpose, to cover his tracks. Though the poem started in the evening, he pushes the "rewind" button and goes back to the "afternoon," which blend into each other to form a barren wasteland of boredom and inaction. But some time has passed in the poem, because earlier he was talking about having tea, and now it seems he has already had tea.

I have seen the moment of my greatness flicker,
And I have seen the eternal Footman hold my coat, and snicker,
And in short, I was afraid. (lines 84-86)

Thought: More time passes in the poem, this time on a larger scale. He comes to realizes that "the moment of my greatness," the moment of his big chance at love, has come and gone. His best chance for happiness is over. Now he only has death, "the eternal Footman," to look forward to. This, he knows, is bad news.

Appearances Quotes
With a bald spot in the middle of my hair –
[They will say: "How his hair is growing thin!"]
My morning coat, my collar mounting firmly to the chin,
My necktie rich and modest, but asserted by a simple pin –
[They will say: "But how his arms and legs are thin!" (lines 40-44)

The Love Song of J. Alfred Prufrock
Shmoop Poetry Guide

Thought: Prufrock is one of those people who is really hard to give a compliment to. "I see you got your collar all the way up to the chin – good for you." "Way to be modest with your necktie – it really just *shouts* 'mediocrity.'" "Your thin arms and legs make the rest of you look so buff!" In short, Prufrock wears the same clothes as everybody else, hoping to blend in and draw attention away from the rest of him. He is a superficial guy who is most concerned with what everyone else (the mysterious "they") will think.

And I have known the eyes already, known them all –
The eyes that fix you in a formulated phrase,
And when I am formulated, sprawling on a pin,
When I am pinned and wriggling on the wall, (lines 55-58)

Thought: When Prufrock looks at other people, he doesn't see complete bodies; he only sees a collection of body parts. Here he sees "the eyes," which treat him like a scientists treats an insect specimen. He misses all the depths and subtleties of human emotion because he has a single-minded focus on the things that make him squirm.

And I have known the arms already, known them all –
Arms that are braceleted and white and bare
[But in the lamplight, downed with light brown hair!]
It is perfume from a dress 65
That makes me so digress?
Arms that lie along a table, or wrap about a shawl. (lines 62-67)

Thought: More body parts. Bring on the arms! We assume these are female arms because they have bracelets, and because Prufrock mostly spends his time thinking about women. But one arm actually catches his eye, and for a brief moment, it seems like it could belong to a real person. The arm is covered with a soft, "light brown hair" that is revealed in the moonlight. If only he could give that much attention to a full person, he might have a richer inner life. But he soon returns to his bored and tired tone.

Shall I part my hair behind? Do I dare to eat a peach?
I shall wear white flannel trousers, and walk upon the beach.
I have heard the mermaids singing, each to each. (lines 122-124)

Thought: Now that he has completely failed to speak up with his question, he is left to worry even more about pointless aspects of his appearance. He considers a change of hairstyle and puts on fancy new pants for his trip to the beach. He focuses on his superficial appearance to cover up for the absence of deep feelings and emotions. And the only beauty he can see is imaginary, like the "mermaids" in the water.

The Love Song of J. Alfred Prufrock
Shmoop Poetry Guide

Study Questions

1. Would you like to go on a walk with Prufrock?
2. How do Guido da Montefeltro and the epigraph from Dante's *Inferno* fit with the rest of the poem? How is Prufrock like Guido? How are they different?
3. Does Prufrock just lead a hellish life, or is he already in Hell? What might make us think that he's actually in Hell?
4. What do you think Prufrock's question is? (Really, tell us, we're dying to know.)
5. Who does Prufrock address his song to? How much do we know about this person?
6. The poem ends with Prufrock drowning with his love in the ocean. Is this ending real or some kind of dream? How does it relate to the rest of the poem? Does it make sense? Is it supposed to?

Did You Know?

Trivia

- One of the possible titles that Eliot didn't use for this poem was "Inventions of the March Hare". (Source)
- Even graffiti vandals in Pennsylvania have been reading Eliot. (Source)
- Prufrock isn't the only one who had trouble with women. Eliot's first marriage to Vivien Eliot was a disaster, and it is rumored that she had an affair with the philosopher Bertrand Russell. (Source)

Steaminess Rating

PG
Things start off racy as we walk through what appears to be a red-light district or some other seedy neighborhood, but Prufrock is too afraid of bodies to show us anything more than a hairy arm.

The Love Song of J. Alfred Prufrock
Shmoop Poetry Guide

Allusions and Cultural References

Literature, Philosophy, and Mythology

- Dante Alighieri, *Inferno*, Canto 27, lines 61-66 (epigraph)
- Andrew Marvell, "To His Coy Mistress" (line 23, first reference)
- Hesiod, *Works and Days* (line 29)
- William Shakespeare, *Twelfth Night* (line 52)
- William Shakespeare, *Hamlet* (lines 111-119)
- The Bible, Luke 16:19-31, (lines 94-95)

Historical References

- Michelangelo (lines 13-14, lines 35-36)
- Lazarus (lines 94-95)

Best of the Web

Videos

Eliot Caught on Tape
http://www.youtube.com/watch?v=Upojbi-6dbM
OK, it's more like a weird animated video where they make Eliot's mouth move.

Prufrock: A Short Film
http://www.youtube.com/watch?v=pgUQxQEESd4&feature=related
It's hard to find videos of this poem that aren't creepy. Here's another one.

Audio

Eliot's Voice
http://www.salon.com/audio/2000/10/05/eliot/
Eliot reads "Prufrock" aloud.

Images

Young Eliot
http://www.artsofinnovation.com/Eliot_at_19.jpg
Here he is. Dashing and disheveled.

Older Eliot

The Love Song of J. Alfred Prufrock
Shmoop Poetry Guide

http://barney.gonzaga.edu/~jmille13/eliot.jpg
Leaning on a cane.

London Fog
http://cuip.net/~stuart/Images/london-fog.jpg
Yes, London really does get foggy, though it's not always yellow.

Historical Documents
A Draft of "Prufrock"
http://classweb.gmu.edu/rnanian/Eliot-Prufrock1911.html
A first draft of "Prufrock," which Eliot started when he was in college in 1911.

Websites
Poets.org
http://www.poets.org/poet.php/prmPID/18
The page on Eliot from the Web site poets.org

Critical Reponses
http://www.english.uiuc.edu/maps/poets/a_f/eliot/prufrock.htm
A bunch of scholars give their interpretations of the poem

Shmoop's Poetry Primer

How to Read Poem

There's really only one reason that poetry has gotten a reputation for being so darned "difficult": it demands your full attention and won't settle for less. Unlike a novel, where you can drift in and out and still follow the plot, poems are generally shorter and more intense, with less of a conventional story to follow. If you don't make room for the *experience*, you probably won't have one.

But the rewards can be high. To make an analogy with rock and roll, it's the difference between a two and a half minute pop song with a hook that you get sick of after the third listen, and a slow-building tour de force that sounds fresh and different every time you hear it. Once you've gotten a taste of the really rich stuff, you just want to listen to it over and over again and figure out: how'd they do that?

Aside from its demands on your attention, there's nothing too tricky about reading a poem. Like anything, it's a matter of practice. But in case you haven't read much (or any) poetry before, we've put together a short list of tips that will make it a whole lot more enjoyable.

- **Follow Your Ears.** It's okay to ask, "What does it mean?" when reading a poem. But it's even better to ask, "How does it sound?" If all else fails, treat it like a song. Even if you can't understand a single thing about a poem's "subject" or "theme," you can always say something – anything – about the sound of the words. Does the poem move fast or slow? Does it sound awkward in sections or does it have an even flow? Do certain words stick out more than others? Trust your inner ear: if the poem sounds strange, it doesn't mean you're reading it wrong. In fact, you probably just discovered one of the poem's secret tricks! If you get stuck at any point, just look for Shmoop's "Sound Check" section. We'll help you listen!

- **Read It Aloud.** OK, we're not saying you have to shout it from the rooftops. If you're embarrassed and want to lock yourself in the attic and read the poem in the faintest whisper possible, go ahead. Do whatever it takes, because reading even part of poem aloud can totally change your perspective on how it works.
- **Become an Archaeologist.** When you've drunk in the poem enough times, experiencing the sound and images found there, it is sometimes fun to switch gears and to become an archaeologist (you know -- someone who digs up the past and uncovers layers of history). Treat the poem like a room you have just entered. Perhaps it's a strange room that you've never seen before, filled with objects or people that you don't really recognize. Maybe you feel a bit like Alice in Wonderland. Assume your role as an archaeologist and take some measurements. What's the weather like? Are there people there? What kind of objects do you find? Are there more verbs than adjectives? Do you detect a rhythm? Can you hear music? Is there furniture? Are there portraits of past poets on the walls? Are there traces of other poems or historical references to be found? Check out Shmoop's "Setting," "Symbols, Imagery, Wordplay," and "Speaker" sections to help you get started.
- **Don't Skim.** Unlike the newspaper or a textbook, the point of poetry isn't to cram information into your brain. We can't repeat it enough: poetry is an experience. If you don't have the patience to get through a long poem, no worries, just start with a really short poem. Understanding poetry is like getting a suntan: you have to let it sink in. When you glance at Shmoop's "Detailed Summary," you'll see just how loaded each line of poetry can be.
- **Memorize!** "Memorize" is such a scary word, isn't it? It reminds us of multiplication tables. Maybe we should have said: "Tuck the poem into your snuggly memory-space." Or maybe not. At any rate, don't tax yourself: if you memorize one or two lines of a poem, or even just a single cool-sounding phrase, it will start to work on you in ways you didn't know possible. You'll be walking through the mall one day, and all of a sudden, you'll shout, "I get it!" Just not too loud, or you'll get mall security on your case.
- **Be Patient.** You can't really understand a poem that you've only read once. You just can't. So if you don't get it, set the poem aside and come back to it later. And by "later" we mean days, months, or even years. Don't rush it. It's a much bigger accomplishment to actually *enjoy* a poem than it is to be able to explain every line of it. Treat the first reading as an investment – your effort might not pay off until well into the future, but when it does, it will totally be worth it. Trust us.
- **Read in Crazy Places.** Just like music, the experience of poetry changes depending on your mood and the environment. Read in as many different places as possible: at the beach, on a mountain, in the subway. Sometimes all it takes is a change of scenery for a poem to really come alive.
- **Think Like a Poet.** Here's a fun exercise. Go through the poem one line at a time, covering up the next line with your hand so you can't see it. Put yourself in the poet's shoes: If I had to write a line to come after this line, what would I put? If you start to think

like this, you'll be able to appreciate all the different choices that go into making a poem. It can also be pretty humbling – at least we think so. Shmoop's "Calling Card" section will help you become acquainted with a poet's particular, unique style. Soon, you'll be able to decipher a T.S. Elliot poem from a Wallace Stevens poem, sight unseen. Everyone will be so jealous.

- **"Look Who's Talking."** Ask the most basic questions possible of the poem. Two of the most important are: "Who's talking?" and "Who are they talking to?" If it's a Shakespeare sonnet, don't just assume that the speaker is Shakespeare. The speaker of every poem is kind of fictional creation, and so is the audience. Ask yourself: what would it be like to meet this person? What would they look like? What's their "deal," anyway? Shmoop will help you get to know a poem's speaker through the "Speaker" section found in each study guide.

- And, most importantly, **Never Be Intimidated.** Regardless of what your experience with poetry in the classroom has been, no poet wants to make his or her audience feel stupid. It's just not good business, if you know what we mean. Sure, there might be tricky parts, but it's not like you're trying to unlock the secrets of the universe. Heck, if you want to ignore the "meaning" entirely, then go ahead. Why not? If you're still feeling a little timid, let Shmoop's "Why Should I Care" section help you realize just how much you have to bring to the poetry table.

Poetry is about freedom and exposing yourself to new things. In fact, if you find yourself stuck in a poem, just remember that the poet, 9 times out of 10, was a bit of a rebel and was trying to make his friends look at life in a completely different way. Find your inner rebel too. There isn't a single poem out there that's "too difficult" to try out – right now, today. So hop to it. As you'll discover here at Shmoop, there's plenty to choose from.

Sources:

http://allpoetry.com/column/2339540
http://academic.reed.edu/writing/paper_help/figurative_language.html
http://web.uvic.ca/wguide/Pages/LiteraryTermsTOC.html#RhetLang
http://www.tnellen.com/cybereng/lit_terms/allegory.html

What is Poetry?

What is poetry? At the most basic level, poetry is an *experience* produced by two elements of language: "sense" and "sound." The "sense" of a word is its meaning. The word "cat" refers to a small, furry animal with whiskers, a long tail, and, if you're unlucky, a knack for scratching up all your new furniture. We can all agree that's what "cat" means. But "cat" also has a particular sound when you say it, and this sound is different from similar words for "cat" in other languages.

Most of the things that you hear, say, or read in your daily life (including the words you are

The Love Song of J. Alfred Prufrock
Shmoop Poetry Guide

reading right now) put more emphasis on meaning than on sound. Not so with poetry. Have you ever repeated a word so many times that it started to sound strange and foreign? No? Try saying that word "cat" twenty times in a row. "Cat, cat, cat, cat, cat, cat . . ." Kind of weird, right? Well, guess what: you just made poetry out of a single word – that is, you turned the word into an experience that is as much about sound as it is about sense. Congratulations, poet!

Or let's imagine that you type the words "blue" and "ocean" on a page all by their lonesome selves. These two little words are quite ordinary and pop up in conversations all the time. However, when we see them isolated, all alone on a page, they might just take on a whole new meaning. Maybe "blue ocean" looks like a little strand of islands in a big sea of white space, and maybe we start to think about just how big the ocean is. Or you could reverse the order and type the words as "ocean blue," which would bring up a slightly different set of connotations, such as everyone's favorite grade-school rhyme: "In 1492 Columbus sailed the ocean blue."

Poetry is also visual, and so it's a good idea to pay attention to how the words are assembled on the page. Our imaginations are often stirred by a poem's visual presentation. Just like a person, poems can send all kinds of signals with their physical appearance. Some are like a slick businessman in a suit or a woman in an evening gown. Their lines are all regularized and divided neatly into even stanzas. Others are like a person at a rock concert who is dressed in tattered jeans, a ragged t-shirt, and a Mohawk, and who has tattoos and piercings all over their body! And some poems, well, some poems look like a baked potato that exploded in your microwave. It's always a good idea to ask yourself how the appearance of words on the page interacts with the meaning of those words. If the poem is about war, maybe it looks like a battle is going on, and the words are fighting for space. If the poem is about love, maybe the lines are spaced to appear as though they are dancing with one another. Often the appearance and meaning will be in total contrast, which is just as interesting.

OK, that's a very broad idea of what poetry is. Let's narrow it down a bit. When most people talk about poetry, they are talking about a particular kind of literature that is broken up into lines, or *verses*. In fact, for most of history, works divided into verse were considered more "literary" than works in prose. Even those long stories called "epics," like Homer's *The Odyssey* and Virgil's *Aeneid*, are actually poems.

Now, you're thinking: "Wait a minute, I thought verses belong to songs and music." Exactly. The very first poets – from Biblical times and even before – set their poems to music, and it's still acceptable to refer to a poem as a "song." For example, the most famous work by the American poet Walt Whitman is titled, "Song of Myself." Because of their shared emphasis on sound, poetry and music have always been like blood brothers.

The last thing to say about poetry is that it doesn't like to be pinned down. That's why there's no single definition that fits all of the things that we would call "poems." Just when you think you have poetry cornered, and you're ready to define it as literature broken into lines, it breaks free and shouts, "Aha! You forgot about the *prose poem*, which doesn't have any verses!" Drats! Fortunately, we get the last laugh, because we can enjoy and recognize poems even without a perfect definition of what poetry is.

Sources:

http://allpoetry.com/column/2339540
http://academic.reed.edu/writing/paper_help/figurative_language.html
http://web.uvic.ca/wguide/Pages/LiteraryTermsTOC.html#RhetLang
http://www.tnellen.com/cybereng/lit_terms/allegory.html

Poetry Glossary

Allegory: An allegory is a kind of extended metaphor (a metaphor that weaves throughout the poem) in which objects, persons, and actions stand for another meaning.

Alliteration: Alliteration happens when words that begin with the same sound are placed close to one another. For example, "the **s**illy **s**nake **s**ilently **s**linked by" is a form of alliteration. Try saying that ten times fast.

Allusion: An allusion happens when a speaker or character makes a brief and casual reference to a famous historical or literary figure or event.

Anaphora: Anaphora involves the repetition of the same word or group of words at the beginning of successive clauses or sections. Think of an annoying kid on a road trip: "Are we there yet? / Are we going to stop soon? / Are we having lunch soon?". Not a poem we'd like to read in its entirety, but the repetition of the word "are" is anaphora.

Anthologize: To put in a poetry anthology, usually for teaching purposes, so that students have a broad selection of works to choose from. Usually, the word will come up in a context like this: "That's one of her most famous poems. I've seen it anthologized a lot." An anthology is a book that has samples of the work of a lot of different writers. It's like a plate of appetizers so you can try out a bunch of stuff. You can also find anthologies for different periods, like Romantic, Modern, and Postmodern. The Norton, Columbia, and Best American anthologies are three of the most famous.

Apostrophe: Apostrophe is when an idea, person, object, or absent being is addressed as if it or they were present, alive, and kicking. John Donne uses apostrophe when he writes this: "Death be not proud, though some have called thee / Mighty and dreadful."

Avant Garde: You'll hear this word used to describe some of the craziest, most far-out, experimental poets. It was originally a French expression that refers to the soldiers who go explore a territory before the main army comes in. Avant garde artists are often people who break through boundaries and do what's never been done before. Then again, sometimes there's a good reason why something has been done before…

Ballad: A ballad is a song: think boy bands and chest-thumping emotion. But in poetry, a ballad is ancient form of storytelling. In the (very) old days, common people didn't get their stories from books – they were sung as musical poems. Because they are meant to convey information, ballads usually have a simple rhythm and a consistent rhyme scheme. They often tell the story of everyday heroes, and some poets, like Bob Dylan, continue to set them to music.

Blank Verse: Thanks to Shakespeare and others, blank verse is one of the most common forms of English poetry. It's verse that has no rhyme scheme but has a regular meter. Usually this meter is iambic pentameter (check out our definition below). Why is blank verse so common in English? Well, a lot of people think we speak in it in our everyday conversations. Kind of like we just did: "a LOT of PEO-ple THINK we SPEAK in IT." That could be a blank verse line.

Cadence: Cadence refers to the rhythmic or musical elements of a poem. You can think of it as the thing that makes poetry sound like poetry. Whereas "meter" refers to the regular elements of rhythm – the beats or accents – "cadence" refers to the momentary variations in rhythm, like when a line speeds up or slows down. Poets often repeat or contrast certain cadences to create a more interesting sound than normal prose.

Caesura: A fancy word for a pause that occurs in the middle of a line of verse. Use this if want to sound smart, but we think "pause" is just fine. You can create pauses in a lot of ways, but the most obvious is to use punctuation like a period, comma, or semicolon. Note that a pause at the end of a line is not a caesura.

Chiasmus: Chiasmus consists of two parallel phrases in which corresponding words or phrases are placed in the opposite order: "Fair is foul, foul is fair."

Cliché: Clichés are phrases or expressions that are used so much in everyday life, that people roll their eyes when they hear them. For example, "dead as a doornail" is a cliché. In good poetry, clichés are never used with a straight face, so if you see one, consider why the speaker might be using it.

Concrete Poetry: Concrete poetry conveys meaning by how it looks on the page. It's not a super-accurate term, and it can refer to a lot of different kinds of poems. One classic example is poems that look like they thing they describe. The French poet Guillaume Apollinaire wrote a poem about Paris in the shape of the Eiffel tower.

Connotation: The suggestive meaning of a word – the associations it brings up. The reason it's not polite to call a mentally-handicapped person "retarded" is that the word has a *negative* connotation. Connotations depend a lot on the culture and experience of the person reading the word. For some people, the word "liberal" has a positive connotation. For others, it's negative. Think of connotation as the murky haze hanging around the literal meaning of a word. Trying to figure out connotations of words can be one of the most confusing and fascinating aspects of reading poetry.

Contradiction: Two statements that don't seem to agree with each other. "I get sober when I drink alcohol" is a contradiction. Some contradictions, like "paradox" (see our definition below), are only apparent, and they become true when you think about them in a certain way.

Denotation: The literal, straightforward meaning of a word. It's "dictionary definition." The word "cat" denotes an animal with four legs and a habit of coughing up furballs.

Dramatic Monologue: You can think of a dramatic monologue in poetry as a speech taken from a play that was never written. Okay, maybe that's confusing. It's a poem written in the voice of a fictional character and delivered to a fictional listener, instead of in the voice of a poet to his or her readers. The British poet Robert Browning is one of the most famous writers of dramatic monologues. They are "dramatic" because they can be acted out, just like a play, and they are monologues because they consist of just one person speaking to another person, just as a "dialogue" consists of two people speaking. (The prefix "mono" means "one," whereas "di" means "two").

Elegy: An elegy is a poem about a dead person or thing. Whenever you see a poem with the title, "In Memory of . . .", for example, you're talking about an elegy. Kind of like that two-line poem you wrote for your pet rabbit Bubbles when you were five years old. Poor, poor Bubbles.

Ellipsis: You see ellipses all the time, usually in the form of "...". An ellipsis involves leaving out or suppressing words. It's like . . . well, you get the idea.

Enjambment: When a phrase carries over a line-break without a major pause. In French, the word means, "straddling," which we think is a perfect way to envision an enjambed line. Here's an example of enjambment from a poem by Joyce Kilmer: 'I think that I shall never see / A poem as lovely as a tree." The sentence continues right over the break with only a slight pause.

Extended metaphor: A central metaphor that acts like an "umbrella" to connect other metaphors or comparisons within it. It can span several lines or an entire poem. When one of Shakespeare's characters delivers an entire speech about how all the world is a stage and people are just actors, that's extended metaphor, with the idea of "theater" being the umbrella connecting everything.

Foot: The most basic unit of a poem's meter, a foot is a combination of long and short syllables. There are all kinds of different feet, such as "LONG-short" and "short-short-LONG." The first three words of the famous holiday poem, "'Twas the Night before Christmas," are one metrical foot (short-short-LONG). By far the most important foot to know is the iamb: short-LONG. An iamb is like one heartbeat: ba-DUM.

Free Verse: "Free bird! Play free bird!" Oops, we meant "Free verse! Define free verse!" Free verse is a poetic style that lacks a regular meter or rhyme scheme. This may sound like free verse has no style at all, but usually there is some recognizable consistency to the writer's use of rhythm. Walt Whitman was one of the pioneers of free verse, and nobody ever had trouble identifying a Whitman poem.

Haiku: A poetic form invented by the Japanese. In English, the haiku has three sections with five syllables, seven syllables, and five syllables respectively. They often describe natural imagery and include a word that reveals the season in which the poem is set. Aside from its three sections, the haiku also traditionally features a sharp contrast between two ideas or images.

The Love Song of J. Alfred Prufrock
Shmoop Poetry Guide

Heroic Couplet: Heroic couplets are rhyming pairs of verse in iambic pentameter. What on earth did this "couplets" do to become "heroic"? Did they pull a cat out of a tree or save an old lady from a burning building? In fact, no. They are called "heroic" because in the old days of English poetry they were used to talk about the trials and adventures of heroes. Although heroic couplets totally ruled the poetry scene for a long time, especially in the 17th and 18th centuries, nowadays they can sound kind of old-fashioned.

Hyperbole: A hyperbole is a gross exaggeration. For example, "tons of money" is a hyperbole.

Iambic Pentameter: Here it is, folks. Probably the single most useful technical term in poetry. Let's break it down: an "iamb" is an unaccented syllable followed by an accented one. "Penta" means "five," and "meter" refers to a regular rhythmic pattern. So "iambic pentameter" is a kind of *rhythmic pattern* that consist of *five iambs* per line. It's the most common rhythm in English poetry and sounds like five heartbeats: ba-DUM, ba-DUM, ba-DUM, ba-DUM, ba-DUM. Let's try it out on the first line of Shakespeare's *Romeo and Juliet*: "In fair Verona, where we lay our scene." Every second syllable is accented, so this is classic iambic pentameter.

Imagery: Imagery is intense, descriptive language in a poem that helps to trigger our senses and our memories when we read it.

Irony: Irony involves saying one thing while really meaning another, contradictory thing.

Metaphor: A metaphor happens when one thing is described as being another thing. "You're a toad!" is a metaphor – although not a very nice one. And metaphor is different from simile because it leaves out the words "like" or "as." For example, a simile would be, "You're *like* a toad."

Metonymy: Metonymy happens when some attribute of what is being described is used to indicate some other attribute. When talking about the power of a king, for example, one may instead say "the crown"-- that is, the physical attribute that is usually identified with royalty and power.

Ode: A poem written in praise or celebration of a person, thing, or event. Odes have been written about everything from famous battles and lofty emotions to family pets and household appliances. What would you write an ode about?

Onomatopoeia: Besides being a really fun word to say aloud, onomatopoeia refers either to words that resemble in sound what they represent. For example, do you hear the hissing noise when you say the word "hiss" aloud? And the old Batman television show *loved* onomatopoeia: "Bam! Pow! Kaplow!"

Oxymoron: An oxymoron is the combination of two terms ordinarily seen as opposites. For example, "terribly good" is an oxymoron.

The Love Song of J. Alfred Prufrock
Shmoop Poetry Guide

Paradox: A statement that contradicts itself and nonetheless seems true. It's a paradox when John Donne writes, "Death, thou shalt die," because he's using "death" in two different senses. A more everyday example might be, "Nobody goes to the restaurant because it's too crowded."

Parallelism: Parallelism happens a lot in poetry. It is the similarity of structure in a pair or series of related words, phrases, or clauses. Julius Caesar's famous words, "I came, I saw, I conquered," are an example of parallelism. Each clause begins with "I" and ends with a verb.

Pastoral: A poem about nature or simple, country life. If the poem you're reading features babbling brooks, gently swaying trees, hidden valleys, rustic haystacks, and sweetly singing maidens, you're probably dealing with a pastoral. The oldest English pastoral poems were written about the English countryside, but there are plenty of pastorals about the American landscape, too.

Personification: Personification involves giving human traits (qualities, feelings, action, or characteristics) to non-living objects (things, colors, qualities, or ideas).

Pun: A pun is a play on words. Puns show us the multiple meanings of a word by replacing that word with another that is similar in sound but has a very different meaning. For example, "when Shmoop went trick-or-treating in a Batman costume, he got lots of snickers." Hehe.

Quatrain: A stanza with four lines. Quatrains are the most common stanza form.

Refrain: A refrain is a regularly recurring phrase or verse especially at the end of each stanza or division of a poem or song. For example in T.S. Eliot's *Love Song for J. Alfred Prufrock*, the line, "in the room the women come and go / Talking of Michelangelo" is a refrain.

Rhetorical Question: Rhetorical questions involve asking a question for a purpose other than obtaining the information requested. For example, when we ask, "Shmoop, are you nuts?", we are mainly expressing our belief that Shmoop is crazy. In this case, we don't really expect Shmoop to tell us whether or not they are nuts.

Rhyming Couplet: A rhyming couplet is a pair of verses that rhyme. It's the simplest and most common rhyme scheme, but it can have more complicated variations (see "Heroic Couplet" for one example).

Simile: Similes compare one thing directly to another. For example, "My love is like a burning flame" is a simile. You can quickly identify similes when you see the words "like" or "as" used, as in "x is like y." Similes are different from metaphors – for example, a metaphor would refer to "the burning flame of my love."

Slam: A form of contemporary poetry that is meant to be performed at informal competitions rather than read. Slam readings are often very political in nature and draw heavily from the rhythms and energy of hip-hop music.

Slant Rhyme: A rhyme that isn't quite a rhyme. The words "dear" and "door" form a slant rhyme. The words sound similar, but they aren't close enough to make a full rhyme.

Sonnet: A well-known poetic form. Two of the most famous examples are the sonnets of William Shakespeare and John Donne. A traditional sonnet has fourteen lines in iambic pentameter and a regular rhyme scheme. Sonnets also feature a "turn" somewhere in the middle, where the poem takes a new direction or changes its argument in some way. This change can be subtle or really obvious. Although we English-speaking folks would love to take credit fort this amazing form, it was actually developed by the Italians and didn't arrive in England until the 16th century.

Speaker: The speaker is the voice *behind* the poem – the person we imagine to be speaking. It's important to note that the speaker is *not* the poet. Even if the poem is biographical, you should treat the speaker as a fictional creation, because the writer is choosing what to say about himself. Besides, even poets don't speak in poetry in their everyday lives – although it would be cool if they did.

Stanza: A division within a poem where a group of lines are formed into a unit. The word "stanza" comes from the Italian word for "room." Just like a room, a poetic stanza is set apart on a page by four "walls" of blank, white space.

Symbol: Generally speaking, a symbol is a sign representing something other than itself.

Synecdoche: In synecdoche a part of something represents the whole. For example: "One does not live by bread alone." The statement assumes that bread is representative of all categories of food.

Syntax: In technical terms, syntax is the study of how to put sentences together. In poetry, "syntax" refers to the way words and phrases relate to each other. Some poems have a syntax similar to everyday prose of spoken English (like the sentences you're reading right now). Other poems have a crazier syntax, where it's hard to see how things fit together at all. It can refer to the order of words in a sentence, like Yoda's wild syntax from the *Star Wars* movies: "A very important concept in poetry, syntax is!" Or, more figuratively, it can refer to the organization of ideas or topics in a poem: "Why did the poet go from talking about his mother to a description of an ostrich?"

Understatement: An understatement seeks to express a thought or impression by underemphasizing the extent to which a statement may be true. Understatement is the opposite of hyperbole and is frequently used for its comedic value in articles, speeches, etc. when issues of great importance are being discussed. Ex: "There's just one, tiny, little problem with that plan – it'll get us all killed!"

Sources:

http://allpoetry.com/column/2339540
http://academic.reed.edu/writing/paper_help/figurative_language.html
http://web.uvic.ca/wguide/Pages/LiteraryTermsTOC.html#RhetLang

http://www.tnellen.com/cybereng/lit_terms/allegory.html

Printed in Great Britain
by Amazon.co.uk, Ltd.,
Marston Gate.